CATHEDRALS

Wordsworth Editions

First published in England 1995 by
Wordsworth Editions Ltd
Cumberland House
Crib Street
Ware
Hertfordshire SG12 9ET

ISBN 1–85326–821–6

*Previous page: **the Nativity scene
from Gaudi's Sagrada Familia,
Barcelona***

Designed and produced by Superlaunch Ltd
P O Box 207, Abingdon, Oxfordshire OX13 6TA, England
Text conversion and pagination by
August Filmsetting, St Helens, England
Colour separation, printing and binding in the
Czech Republic by Svoboda

CONTENTS

INTRODUCTION

I have always headed for the city rail station on arrival; however, when compiling this volume I have been forced to rethink, and now recommend making straight for the cathedral. This is almost always in the oldest part of the city, if no longer its centre; the ancient street patterns, aged buildings and bustling traditional open markets which surround it frequently offer the most pleasant and traffic free amenities for the urban tourist.

To the believer, the cathedral provides a focus for faith and a target for pilgrimage. As in medieval times, to most of us it simply remains the finest building, reflecting centuries of history in its structure and so embodying the very essence of the city in which it stands.

Cathedrals demonstrate the peak of architectural output, having been built ostensibly for the glory of God but thus permitting their creators to give of their best craftsmanship and technical daring. They stand as monument to a staggering commitment of time, skill and money. Built by the foremost craftsmen of the day, who took pride in employing the most up to date building techniques, because they were also dependent on a constant flow of finance, many took decades to complete. The ambitions of their bishops or congregations gave rise to some daring experimentation, as did the lack of technique of earlier builders, which sometimes forced innovative solutions upon their successors. These factors have rendered our great churches unmatched for the variety of their construction, and totally unapproachable both for their beauty and the quality of the craftsmanship, be it in stone, glass or wood. So simple in plan, the architecture of a cathedral is transmuted by the skills of its builders and the aspirations of its congregation into an awe-inspiring achievement which reflects hundreds of years of Christian striving.

Unfortunately there is not enough space to cover either every building or the complete history of those included. Instead these major examples offer a starting point for enjoyment and learning about the beautiful places that make up our cultural heritage and add to our understanding.

Right: *the Cathedral at Roermond, the Netherlands, overlooks the river on the west, and has a small bustling market in the square behind it*

MAIN CHURCH BUILDING STYLES

In chronological order, these are:

Saxon: the building style in Britain before the Norman Conquest (1066), smaller scale and less developed decoratively than Norman, but otherwise quite similar

Norman/Romanesque: typically has rounded arches, simple vaulting, vigorously carved detail; it was introduced into Britain around the time of the Norman Conquest, and lasted until 1150

Transitional: the term usually used for 12th century buildings which combine Norman and Early English elements, such as when round and pointed arches appear together

Gothic: the style of most of the medieval period, characterised by pointed arches and generally with ever increasing emphasis through the period on vertical elements, giving more height and light

Early English: the first style of English Gothic, between about 1150 and 1250, typically having lancet windows and decorative dogtooth moulding

Decorated: the second phase of English Gothic, between about 1250 and 1350, with more elaborate carving on columns and Geometric window tracery

Perpendicular: the most fully evolved form of English Gothic, between about 1350-1550, having sophisticated vaulting systems and using large windows and vertical elements to create lightness and spaciousness

Flamboyant: the southern European Gothic style, from the 14th century onwards; it was contemporary with English Perpendicular and is most easily recognisable at its apogee in the petal-shaped tracery of rose windows

Baroque: elaborate and finely finished architecture inspired by the buildings of ancient Greece and Rome, which developed from the Renaissance style in Rome in the 16th century. It was fully developed a century later, but took longer to become established every where else in Europe. The mathematical advances of the time enabled architects to create solid and dignified structures showing a controlled energy

Gothic Revival: an English movement of the Victorian age combining architectural and religious fervour, its style based on imitations of medieval churches, especially of the Early English period

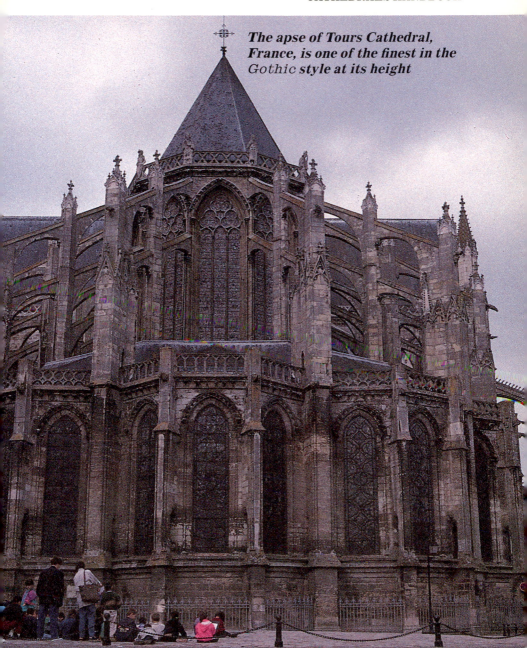

The apse of Tours Cathedral, France, is one of the finest in the Gothic style at its height

CATHEDRAL PLANS A typical cathedral plan

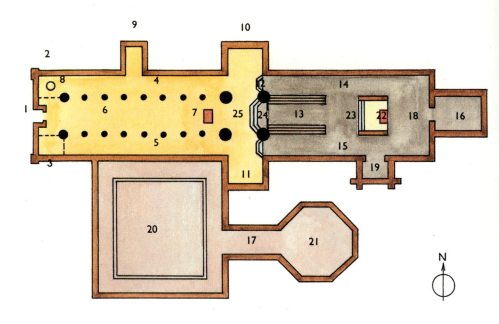

KEY

1	west door
2	NW tower over
3	SW tower over
4	north aisle
5	south aisle
6	nave
7	nave altar
8	baptistery and font
9	entrance porch
10	north transept
11	south transept

12	steps
13	choir
14	north choir aisle
15	south choir aisle
16	Lady Chapel
17	vestibule
18	retrochoir
19	side chapel
20	cloister
21	chapter house
22	High Altar
23	sanctuary
24	choir screen
25	crossing (tower over)

A section through a cathedral

KEY

		7	aisle
		7	aisle
1	flying buttress	8	roof space
2	boss	8	roof space
3	vault	9	roof construction
4	rib	10	arcade
5	shaft	11	triforium
6	nave	12	clerestory

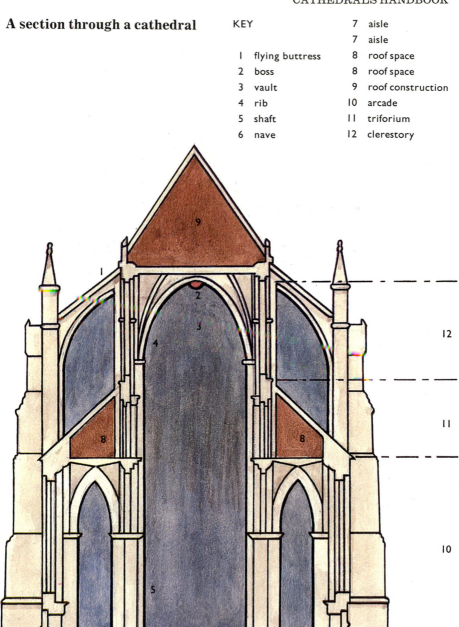

9

GLOSSARY

aisle: the outer part of the church; the aisles run parallel with and on both sides of the nave or chancel, and are separated from it by an arcade. Generally the roof is lower over the aisles, with the nave walls above the level of the aisle roofs being pierced by the clerestory windows. The aisles are mainly used for seating and the memorial tombs may be sited there

almonry: the place where help was given to the poor and sick

altar: the altar is the communion table, used for the bread and wine. It is often the focal point of the church building

altarpiece: situated behind the altar, this is an ornamental panel, often with a painting

ambo: a raised lectern, most common in medieval Italian churches, from which the Bible was read

ambulatory: passageway behind the High Altar, leading from one side of the church to the other, and used for processions. It was especially useful for pilgrim churches, for 'walking round'

apse: the vaulted semicircular or polygonal east end of a church or chapel, typical of the Norman period

arcade: a row of arches carried on columns or piers, separating

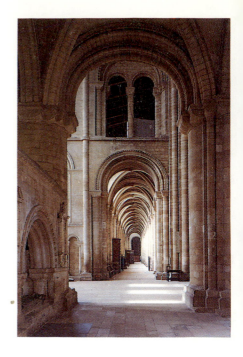

The south nave aisle, *Peterborough Cathedral, England*

An altarpiece *from Beauvais, France*

Bourges Cathedral, France; an arcade of arches with stained glass behind

Inside the ancient baptistery at Aix-en-Provence, France

the nave or chancel from an aisle

arch: a curving structural support between two piers or columns

ashlar: smooth squared blocks of stone; also known as **dressed stone**

aumbry: a cupboard or recess used for storage of the sacramental vessels, the cups and plates used in the Eucharist

baldacchino: a large ornamental canopy placed over an altar or tomb and usually supported on columns

ball-flower: form of stone ornamentation from the Decorated style of building, the motif consisting of a three-petalled flower enclosing a small ball

baptistery: the part of a church used for baptisms, housing the font

barrel vault: a early form of vault with a semi-cylindrical roof

basilica: a style of church that consisted of a nave and two or more lower and narrower aisles

bay: a single arch in an arcade, or a section of wall between pillars, or one set of vault ribs; the smallest unit of a building

belfry: the part of the tower where the bells are hung

bells: a full peal of bells weighs several tonnes, and adds considerable stress to the tower. In Britain, change ringing of six or

The belfry at the south transept at Palencia Cathedral, Spain

The St Peter bell at Köln Cathedral, Germany

more bells is practised, when bells are rung manually in intricately varying sequences, whereas in continental Europe mechanical **carillons** are widely used to chime the bell

bema: a raised platform, widely used in the early churches, on which the preacher stood to speak

blind arcade: a line of arches used as a decorative feature, which were not free standing but had a solid wall surface behind

boss: an ornamental knob of wood or stone, which was used to cover the intersection of two or more ribs in a vault or of the roof timbers

buttress: masonry or brickwork which, by being built against a wall, gave added support and a greater rigidity to the whole structure. The massive buttresses of the Norman churches left little room for large windows, while the Gothic style placed buttresses only at key structural points

candelabrum: a multiple candle holder, which is suspended from the ceiling

candles: the larger churches were often difficult to light, and gigantic candlesticks began to appear about 1100. Candlepower or illumination power is rated in terms of a 22mm ($\frac{7}{8}$in) sperm candle burning at the rate of 120

grains per hour

capital: a decorative crown to a column, below the arch. They are usually carved with foliage, figures, patterns or all three

carillon: *see* **bells**

carrel: a recessed seat in a cloister wall, used by monks as a place of study

cathedral: the principal church of a diocese, in which is the seat of the bishop; its derivation is from the Greek word *kathĕdra*, a seat

cenotaph: a sepulchral monument to one who is buried elsewhere

chamfer: bevelled without moulding

chancel: the eastern end of a church, beyond the crossing. The main altar is placed there, and it is often reserved for the clergy and choir

chantry: a small chapel or an endowment where the priest chants masses. They were commissioned in the Middle Ages by the wealthy for the chanted intercession on behalf of the souls of the members of their families who had died. Today they are used for private prayer or smaller services

chapel: small chapels are often built off the eastern wall of the transepts and on side aisles; many are **chantry chapels**

chapter house: an assembly room in which the dean and the

A small side chapel at Lisieux Cathedral, France

canons, who form the chapter of a cathedral, meet for the discussion of business

chevet: a French term referring to the east end of a church that consists of several apsidal chapels

chevron: a Norman (Romanesque) decoration in the form of a zig-zag

choir *also* **quire:** the part of a church which is between the presbytery and nave and contains stalls, which are often the most impressive seating in the church, and from which the services are sung

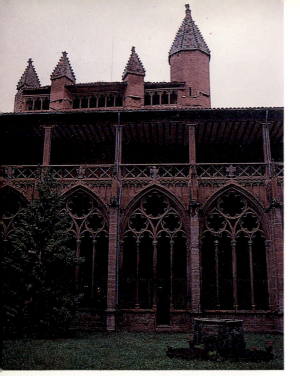

The cloisters *at* ***Pamplona, Spain***

choir screen: *see* **pulpitum**

churrigeresque: a highly decorated late Baroque style in Spain

cinquefoil: five-leaved

clerestory: the upper level of a church wall, pierced by windows which are set above the line of the aisle roofs and thus provide light to the centre of the building

cloister: an external quadrangle with a covered walk all round and with monastic offices which open off it

close *or* **precinct:** the cathedral surroundings; in England these usually comprise a grassy area around the cathedral, and are bordered by the bishop's palace, the deanery and other accommodation

collegiate: a church which has a college of priests or a chapter, but not a bishop

column: a vertical, generally tapered, load-bearing shaft with circular cross-section

compound pier: a cluster of shafts which may not be joined, but which provide upright support

confessional *or* **confession boxes:** a common feature of Roman Catholic churches, where the priest sits and listens through a

The crypt *at* ***Bayeaux, France***

14

*A cupola **at Siena Cathedral, Italy***

...all aperture to those who ...ish to make their confessions ...order to be given penance and ...hus absolution

consistory court: a bishop's court, which has jurisdiction over church matters

corbel: a projecting stone bracket, often ornamented, which provides support for a beam or roof vaulting

cornice: projecting decorative moulding at the upper part of a wall at roof level or sur-mounting a column

crocket: a small richly carved and decorated projection on spires and pinnacles

crossing: the central space in a church, which is usually sur-mounted by a central tower. It is the intersection of the main east-west axis of the nave, where the church is crossed by the north-south transept

cruciform: having the shape of a cross

crypt: the church basement; it is usually sited at the east end and is often vaulted; it is used for services and for burials

cupola: small ornamental dome

cusp: a sill or small projection on the underside of a window arch, dividing it into leaves (foils)

diaper: decoration in a diamond pattern

diocese *or* **see:** collective term for the parishes of a cathedral and its bishop

dogtooth: an Early English ornamental pattern of small pyramid or star-like shapes

dome: a vault built on a circular base

doors: cathedral west front doors were reserved for proces-sions, religious festivals and State occasions, while most day to day visitors passed through a doorway on the north west aisle. The doors were pro-tected from the weather by a **porch**

15

*Effigies **of bishops in Bayeaux Cathedral, France***

dressed stone: *see* **ashlar**
drum: the round vertical wall which supports a dome
effigy: a portrait statue, usually of wood or stone, and which usually lies on the top of a tomb
elevation: the front, back or sides of a building, viewed from directly in front
engaged shaft: *see* **half shaft**
entablature: the uppermost part of the order which surmounts a column and comprises a cornice, frieze and architrave
facing: finishing material which is applied to the outer surface of a wall
fan vault: vaulting in a fan like pattern, usually creating a lacy appearance; it dates from the Perpendicular period, and was widely used in the 14th century
feretory: an ornamental setting placed behind the High Altar for the main shrine
fillet: the flat narrow band in between mouldings
finial: the ornament at the very

*Fan vaulting, **Peterborough Cathedral, England***

tip of a spire or canopy
flèche: a French term for a small spire
flushwork: a decorative combination of flint and dressed stone, used to form a pattern when building a wall
flying buttress: external buttresses or strengthening arches, which stretch from a vertical buttress to a wall, generally the upper wall of the nave. Their purpose is to counteract the outward thrust of the roof against the relatively thin upper nave walls
foliate: leaf like
font: used for baptism. It contains holy water, which is sprinkled on those being baptised as a symbol of the washing

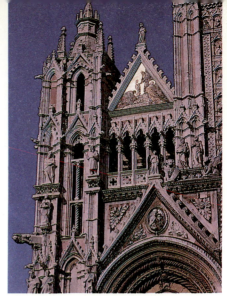

*A font **by Onofré Julià, 1433, in Barcelona Cathedral, Spain***

away of sins. The font was virtually always near the church entrance in medieval times, to symbolise the entry into the family of God

frater: the dining room of the monastery

freestone: a fine grained stone which can easily be cut and worked

frontal: covering for the front of an altar

galilee *or* **narthex:** originally the porch at the west end of a church, sometimes enlarged to form a chapel

gallery *or* **tribune:** the upper storey inside the church and above the aisle. It is open to the nave, and in Italy is known as the **loggia**

gargoyle: a projecting water spout used as a means of taking away rain water from the roof quickly, while keeping it from the walls. If water overflows onto the walls or the vault, it might cause rot or, in the last stage, collapse. The gargoyle

*Gargoyles **seem to spring out from the northwest corner of Siena Cathedral, Italy***

was fixed to the guttering as the simplest way of removing the water and of letting it fall clear of the walls. The word is derived from the French *gargouille*, meaning throat, and as a disguise, these spouts commonly assumed the form of birds, beasts (often mythic) and later on human heads or sometimes even portraits

garth: the area enclosed by a cloister

Geometric: the early type of Gothic tracery which was based on geometric forms, usually circles and triangles

grisaille: greyish patterned glass, usually in small lozenge shapes

groin: the intersecting edge between two planes of a vault

hagioscope: *see* **squint**

half shaft *or* **engaged shaft:** a column partially attached to, or sunken into, a wall

hammer beam: a projecting bracket that supports the main trusses of a roof

heart shrine: a shrine, usually quite small, that holds the heart of a saint or that of a noble

hood mould *or* **label:** weathering used to protect the upper edge of a door or window

icon: an image of a saint, apostle or martyr, used most often in Eastern churches as an aid to the worship of God

iconoclasm: the smashing of icons

iconostasis: a screen separating the nave from the sanctuary in a Byzantine church. It usually has three doors, and is decorated with icons

Jesse tree: the family tree which shows the descent of Christ from Jesse, the father of King David. In cathedrals, this is a very popular subject for stained glass windows

keystone: the central stone in an arch or rib

label: *see* **hood mould**

Lady Chapel: a chapel dedicated to the Virgin Mary; usually sited at the east end of a church

lancet: a narrow window, with a

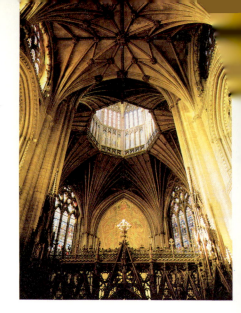

The 14th century octagonal wooden lantern of Ely Cathedral, England

The lectern in the choir of Salamanca Cathedral holds one of the Cathedral's many music manuscripts

ointed arch; typically Early English

lantern: a circular or polygonal tower with windows all round, most usually above the church crossing

lavatorium: the trough with running water provided, often outside the frater doorway, where monks could wash their hands before meals

lectern: a reading desk on a stand from which Bible lessons can be read. It is often in the form of a brass eagle, which has spread wings to support the Bible

lierne: the tertiary linking ribs in a vault

lights: the subdivisions of a complex window

lintel: a horizontal beam cut from timber or stone

loggia: *see* **gallery**

martyrion: a memorial or church building which has been constructed over the grave of a martyr

memorial tombs: a feature of many old church buildings, these have resulted from the practice of burying the most influential persons within the church building. Carved stone tombs and decorated brasses mark their burial places

Merovingian: the first Merovingian king was Clovis, crowned at Reims in 496, but little now remains of their architecture

minster: there is no precise definition of this term, but it is applied to a church of importance, which is not necessarily a cathedral

misericord: the bracket under a hinged seat in the choir stall provided for monks to lean against, to give support during long periods of standing

monstrance: the receptacle in which the consecrated Host is exposed for adoration

moulding: an ornamental contour given to the stones of arches. The moulding is sometimes cut from contrasting stone, the horizontal divisions being emphasised with thin mouldings known as stringing

mudéjar: Moorish style of the Muslims who remained in Christian Spain after the Reconquest

mullion: a vertical bar of wood or stone dividing the lights of a window

narthex *see* **galilee**

nave: that part of the church which extends west from the crossing and is separated from the side aisles by arcading. It is the main area for the congregation. In medieval times, it was used as a popular meeting place and even used for trading

octafoil: eight leaved

ogee: alternating concave and convex curves forming an S shape, common in Decorated

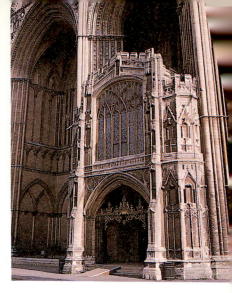

The nave *looking towards the* **apse of Nantes Cathedral, France**

The west front porch *of* **Peterborough Cathedral, England**

period arches, and Byzantine or Orthodox churches

ogival: term for a style of architecture using pointed arches; Gothic

order: the combination of the columns, base, capitals and entablature which had been developed in ancient times and copied in the classical revival; the Greek orders include Doric, Ionic and Corinthian

parclose: a screen separating a chapel from the rest of the church, usually wooden

parvise: a room which was built over a porch

pediment: a gently pitched gable, which was sited over a portico

pendant: an elongated roof boss, which gives the appearance of

hanging down

pentise: a lean-to which is used to form a passageway

pews: wooden bench seating, provided for the congregation and a dominant feature in many church buildings, although owing to their inflexibility some churches now prefer chairs. It was not a common practice to sit in church until the 15th century. Pews began to appear with the Reformation, arranged in a semi-circle around the pulpit. These were later fixed to the floor. By the 18th century, pews were being sold to families, who often regarded them as private property

pier: a solid vertical main sup-

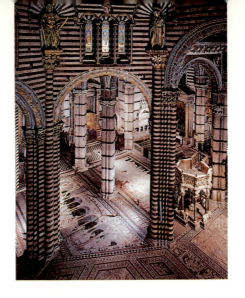

port for arcades, most often with a square cross section

pilaster: a shallow and flattened column projecting from a wall

pinnacle: a small top to a spire or buttress, like a tower

piscina: a small basin sited in a wall niche near to the altar and used for washing sacramental vessels

plinth: projecting masonry, sometimes with a decorative moulding, at the base of a wall

Plateresque: the rich style of surface decoration, supposed to be similar to silversmiths' work, of the 16th century

podium: the base or platform on which a tomb or statue stands

porch: built to protect a doorway from the weather, the porch took on its own significance, being used in medieval times to conduct marriages and also for arranging business deals by the church door. Porch sculpture usually takes on two themes, the baptism of Christ (a symbol of entry into God's family, the Church) and the four seasons, as a reminder that God is involved in all parts of human labours

portico: grandiose porch, with its roof supported on columns, usually protecting the main west entrance

precinct: *see* **close**

presbytery: that part of a church, east of the choir, that is

A view from the triforium of Siena Cathedral, Italy, looking down on Pisano's pulpit

reserved for the clergy and which houses the main altar

pulpit: the place from which the preaching of the Word of God takes place. A main focal point, usually placed along one side of the arcade; with the new emphasis on preaching during the Reformation, the pulpit was increased to great heights so that the preacher could address the gallery in addition to those at floor level. Stairs lead up to two or three levels, the lower level platforms being used for the announcements and readings only, the uppermost for preaching

pulpitum *or* **choir screen:** a partition between the nave and choir, used to emphasise the mystery and holiness of the service in Catholic churches; normally it is of stone, but also sometimes may be beautifully carved wood

pyx: the container in which consecrated bread is kept for the Eucharist

quatrefoil: four leaved

quire: *see* **choir**

quoins: dressed stones at the corners of a building, usually slightly protruding from the wall face

rebus: the punning visual representation of a word or especially name, famously the arrow (bolt) and barrel (tun) of Bolton

Reformation: the religious upheaval of the 16th century which gave rise to the formation of the various Protestant churches

reredos *or* **retable:** ornamental screen placed behind the altar

respond: a half column or half capital at the juncture of an arch or arcade and a wall

retable: *see* **reredos**

reticulated: window tracery made to look like a net

retrochoir: the part of a church situated immediately behind the choir

rib: a projecting part of the stone framework, usually load bearing, and which supports a vaulted roof

rood: an old Saxon word for

The retable *at* Ávila, Spain

Milan Cathedral's roof *is an ideal point from which to appreciate many of the Cathedral's 2,245 sculpted figures*

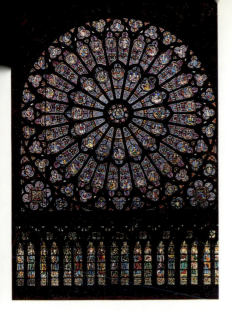

*A beautiful rose window **from Nôtre Dame, Paris***

Chichester has the only English cathedral** spire **visible from the sea, at 84.4m (277ft)

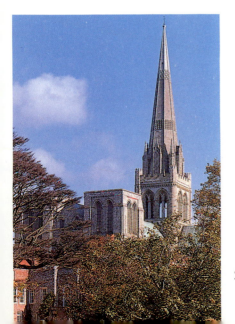

cross

rood screen: a transverse screen separating the chancel from the nave, generally of wood and pierced with tracery and surmounted by a crucifix (rood)

roof: cathedral roofs are most often covered in plate lead of up to 7mm ($\frac{1}{4}$in) thick, which adds considerably to the weight and stress on the walls. Therefore, a carefully cross braced beam structure lies between the vault and the roof cladding

rose window: a circular window with a tracery of stone that radiates from its centre

sacristy: a room where sacred vessels and vestments are stored

sanctuary: an area at the east end of the church, within the communion rail, containing the altar

sarcophagus: an elaborately carved coffin

sedilia: seats for the clergy, generally three in number, for officiating priests, built into the south wall of the chancel and often elaborately carved

see: *see* **diocese**

sexfoil: six leaved

shaft: a small subordinate pillar

shrine: the housing of a saint's body or other relics

soffit: the underside of an arch or window head

spire: a tall conical or polygonal structure, topping a

tower. Not all churches have spires, although the spire is said to represent a symbol of man's aspiration to be united with his Creator. They are often a symbol of local pride, in addition to being a signpost for travellers

springer: the lowest stone of an arch or vaulting rib

squinch: arches placed diagonally across the corner of an intersection of walls to carry a tower

squint *or* **hagioscope:** this is more commonly known as a **leper's squint**, a slanted aperture cut through the stone work, to provide a view of the High Altar

stalls: facing rows of carved wooden seats, which line the walls of the choir or chancel

steeple: a combination of tower and spire

stellar: a star-like pattern often formed by the ribs in a vault

stiff-leaf: Early English carving of formalised foliage on capitals

stoup: the basin at a church's entrance, which contains holy water

strainer arch: an arch reinforced with bolts or canvas strapping

string course: a horizontal band of stonework which may project from the wall

tabernacle: a recess or ornamental receptacle for relics or the sacraments used in the Eucharist

tesselated: small tiles cut into squares and laid out to form mosaic work

tierceron: a secondary rib that rises from the base of a vault and reaches the ridge

tower: a huge tower increases the church's visibility, and in addition supports the (often incredibly heavy) bells. Cathedrals may have up to nine towers, but the most common arrangements are either a single tower at the west end, or two towers, one on each side of the west front and with a third large tower at the crossing. A central tower is used to represent the church's contact between heaven and earth

tracery: ornamental stone ribwork in the head of a window; also applied to woodwork in a screen

transept: the transverse part of a cruciform church, running north-south

trefoil: three leaved

triforium *or* **tribune:** the middle level of the nave, between the main arcade of the church and the clerestory

tribune: *see* **gallery**

triptych: a work of art in three parts, hinged so that the two smaller outer parts fold over the larger central one. Each part is related to the others in

The tower of Antwerp Cathedral reaches 123m (403ft 6in)

subject, treatment and context
tympanum: a panel, usually very decorative, between the lintel and the door arch
undercroft: a vaulted chamber supporting a main chamber such as a **frater**
vault: arched work forming a stone or wooden roof. The vault is always one of the most spectacular interior elements of a church, and may range from the crudely hewn tunnel vaults of the early Romanesque period to the very impressive pendulum vaults of the 17th century. The first rib vaults from the 12th century were purely functional

but ribs were soon added for decorative effect in addition to their structural relevance
vesica: a pointed oval
vestry: a room used by the clergy and choir for changing into their ceremonial robes
voussoir: a single stone of an arch
west front: this is the single most considered feature of the exterior and often the most elaborately designed part of a church; a façade incorporating the large entrance doors, very symbol of the gate to heaven. In the 11th century, the west end was divided into three vertical sections which indicated the internal divisions of a nave with an aisle either side. A single large window invariably filled the upper central part

The west front of Cremona Cathedral, with its clock tower on the left

Aachen, Germany

Charlemagne established his personal chapel in Aachen in 798, on the ruins of an ancient Roman baths. This chapel was also designed to become his personal mausoleum, and was modelled after the church of San Vitale in Ravenna, since when a series of additions and embellishments have turned the building into a three dimensional mirror of the history of German church architecture.

The chapel became a cathedral in 1801, and contains some of Christendom's most adored treasures, including the swaddling clothes of the infant Jesus, the cloak worn by the Virgin at the Nativity, and what was thought to have been the loin cloth that Jesus wore when He was crucified; all of which are publicly displayed every seven years for a two-week period.

The nucleus of the present Cathedral, the astoundingly richly embellished octagonal chapel built for Charlemagne in the Byzantine style by the master architect Otto, has served as the coronation chapel

The entrance to Aachen Cathedral is via the Wolf's Door under the front tower, and is reached from the Domhof (Cathedral court)

for several German emperors. The Emperor's Throne is located in the gallery, but may only be visited with a guide. The entrance to Aachen Cathedral is via the Wolf's Door, under the front tower, and this is reached from the Domhof (Cathedral court).

Albrecht Dürer wrote that in Aachen he had seen the 'well proportioned columns with their fine porphyry capitals of green and red gutterstone' installed by Charlemagne, and that he had seen there 'all sorts of magnificent treasures, unlike any ... which we living may see today.'

Aix-en-Provence, France

The beauty of the fine detail of the Cathedral outshines the overall design and construction, which is partly Gothic and partly Romanesque, yet it contains practically every phase of Provençal architecture. Many centuries of building are also evident, with an 11th century south aisle, 12th century cloisters and an excellent 13th century nave; added to all of which is a mainly 15th century façade. The inner walls are adorned by Flemish tapestries of the 15th and 16th centuries;

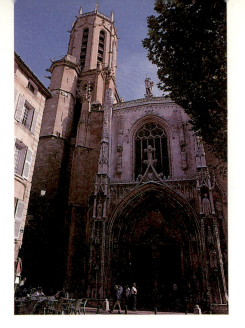

The Cathedral at Aix-en-Provence quietly nestles amid narrow streets, making it difficult to locate, and it does not force its presence upon the populace

those in the choir depict the Passion and life of the Virgin.

Among the most important works of art to be found in the Cathedral is a triptych of Moses and the burning bush, painted by Nicolas Froment between 1475 and 1476.

Right: *the tympanum of the west front porch depicts Christ in Majesty holding the Book of Life, flanked by the symbols of the Four Evangelists*

Angers, France

The west front has a striking 12th century façade consisting of a portal with its Norman arch, the first storey with its stained glass windows and blind arcades, and the two square towers with their 15th century steeples of finely wrought stone. The central Renaissance tower was added in the 16th century.

Inside there is an aisleless nave, a 12th century architectural masterpiece; the walls, columns and round headed windows are Norman, yet the convex vaults, with their four ribs, anticipate the emerging Gothic style.

The High Altar is a golden glory in Baroque style from the mid 18th century, while the panelling in the chancel is slightly later, and shows subjects of the Old Testament on

the south side, and of the New Testament on the north side.

Angers cathedral possesses the most precious collection of tapestries known. Of these the most famous is *The Revelation* which is the largest tapestry in the world; however, this has recently been removed and can now be seen in the castle, but this still leaves hundreds more, and many are still hung in the Cathedral.

Above: *a view of the nave of Ávila Cathedral*

Ávila, Spain

The early Gothic cathedral of Ávila was begun in about 1157, and is a grim reminder of the time when Christians and Moors contended for power in Spain. It was built to repel the seiges of the infidels; the great battlemented apse, built from about 1160 to 1180 by Maestro Fruchel, forms a bastion in the city's medieval wall.

The Cathedral is a genuine survivor, a relic from a savage world. It is built in cold dark grey stone, with an internal solemnity that is celebrated throughout Spain. Its length measures 96.9m (318ft), it has a breadth of 50m (164ft) with a nave spanning 8.5m (28ft), and stands 25m (82ft) high. The choir was built at the very end of the 12th century, and is influenced by the choir at Vézelay.

The nave appears somewhat narrow, with a blind triforium and a large clerestory. There is some impressive glass dating from the 15th century which is in the main chapel, the work of Juan de Valdivielso, and an admirable *retable major*, the work of Pedro Berraguete and two other Spanish painters, in between 1499 and 1508. It shows SS Peter and Paul with evangelists, doctors and scenes from the life of Christ and the Passion. The Cathedral was completed in 1547, when the stalls were finished.

Above: *Barcelona's Catedral de Santa Eulàlia, with its delicate spires*

Inset: *Gaudi's unfinished Holy Family Church is an extravagant* *epitaph to one man's genius and to his faith. Construction work is kept going by donations but the unimaginable culmination of his life's work must still be some lifetimes in the future*

Barcelona, Spain

On the top of a hill in the centre of the picturesque medieval quarter stands the Cathedral of Barcelona. It is thought to be the probable site of a pagan temple, but with the city's rise to dominance in the western Mediterranean, a later house of Christian worship was built on the site. This was partially destroyed by the Moors in the tenth century, only to be rebuilt from 1046 to 1058, as a Romanesque church. It was raised again at the end of the 13th century, and the present Cathedral was begun in 1298 by the architect Beltrán Riquer and was mostly completed by the middle of the 15th century, with the exception of the upper and lower stalls and the elaborately decorated west front, which was not built until the 1890s.

The Cathedral is confined on three sides by narrow streets, but cleverly thought out floodlighting at night creates a wonderful effect. This is enhanced by internal lighting from behind the stained-glass windows, which are themselves a good example of late Gothic stained glass. Barcelona Cathedral is very dark inside, with small windows which are placed high and give an eerie glow. The High Altar is raised high above the general floor level and there are many side chapels around the apse, filled with treasures, altarpieces and fittings which were saved from destruction between 1931 and 1939. These represent an incomparable treasury of medieval art and an insight into the church of the Middle Ages. The crypt below the High Altar is entered from the west via an open flight of stairs.

The Cathedral's cloister, which was built by the architect Bernard Roca between 1382 and 1448, is remarkable for its irregular arches and its many unconventional capitals, and is one of the finest in Europe.

Bayeux, France

The Cathedral at Bayeux was dedicated in 1077 by Bishop Eudes de Conteville, who was the half brother of William the Conqueror, and is regarded as one of the finest examples of Norman architecture. In contrast to the sombre exterior, the Romanesque nave is exceptionally well illuminated by a group of high windows above the triforium.

The chapter house's 12th century arches were rebuilt in the

Above: *the pulpit and above the clear windows of the triforium through which the flying buttresses can be seen*

4th century, and are supported by brackets decorated with monsters. Bayeux's façade is flanked by Romanesque towers, and was reinforced by large buttresses in the 13th century when the spires were added. The central tower is 15th century.

The Cathedral contains 22 chapels and a west window of 15th century glass, presented by the Guild of Cooks. This is, however, now obscured by the organ. The carving on the tympanum of the south portal vividly depicts the history of St Thomas Becket and those of the two side portals, the Last Judgment and the Passion.

The apse, seen here from the south side, gives no indication of the immense amount of work underway in Beauvais' naveless cathedral

Beauvais, France

The Bishop of Beauvais, Milou de Nanteuil, was envious of the emergent Cathedral at Amiens, about 45km (30 miles) to the north of Beauvais, and had plans drawn up for his own cathedral, which was to surpass all others in height and beauty. Work began immediately, but with the apse hardly finished, in 1284 because of a combination of weak buttressing and poor foundations, the vaulting had crumbled and the roof fell in.

The Cathedral was rebuilt, more slowly and more solidly, but was then interrupted by, among various other things, the Hundred Years' War. It was 1500 when the stone was laid for the transepts, and in order to elicit donations, the Bishop permitted the populace who did

donate to eat butter and cheese during Lent.

Once again, Beauvais pride was challenged with the rising in Rome of the dome of St Peter's, and so the Bishop sold off Cathedral treasures to raise funds for a spire to rise 150m (492ft) above the Cathedral pavement; this is 12.2m (40ft) higher than the dome of St Peter's. St Peter's, Beauvais, was then able to boast of the highest cathedral in the world, but this was short lived. It was completed in the autumn of 1569; the spire was a graceful, elegant stone stem with a *flèche* of oak topped by an iron cross, which all proved too much. The structure crumbled just after the congregation had departed on Ascension Day, 1573. Today repair work to the nave is finally underway.

The interior contains a series of remarkable tapestries that date from the 15th, 16th and 17th centuries; two famous clocks from the 14th and 19th centuries respectively, and Beauvais is still able to boast the highest Gothic chancel in the world, at some 47m (154ft).

Bourges, France

St Etienne's Cathedral is a splendid masterpiece of Gothic

Right: *Bourges Cathedral seen from the Archbishop's Garden*

architecture. Its structure, contrary to the vast majority of other great churches of the same period, was designed and built in one great phase, rather than in successive stages over many years. The plans of the Maître of Bourges drawn up around 1195 favoured perspectives, light, and space; this is what captivates whoever may enter Bourges Cathedral nave for the first time and makes it a symbol of the golden age of Gothic architecture.

The absence of a transept enables the eye to take in the entire interior. The crypt, the largest in France, and the most splendidly designed, has served as a church within a church. This lower church was part of the initial building work from 1195 to 1215, along with the chevet and choir. The nave and the main façade formed the second half of the construction programme, the whole being completed by 1260. The south tower had to be supported by a high buttressing pier at the start of the 14th century, and so the consecration had to be delayed until 1324.

The façade, which boasts five portals of varying size and shape, a great central gable, a

pedestal of 15 graceful steps and Dammartin's huge central window, remains as one of the unquestioned masterpieces of the Gothic era. The Cathedral itself was recognised in 1992 by UNESCO, when it was placed on its list of World Heritage Monuments.

Bristol, England

Originally the church of an abbey founded in 1140, this is a rare example of a hall church, ie the aisle, nave and choir are of equal height with the pier arches rising to the full height of the building, which is without triforium or clerestory. The abbey church became the Cathedral of the new see of Bristol in 1542.

Particularly important is the choir vault, which has no ridge rib but centres on a series of open compartments and the choir itself, which is in early Decorated style, unparalleled elsewhere; it has the earliest lierne vaulting in England and the foliage capitals are of outstanding beauty.

The Cathedral's eastern part, last rebuilt in the early 14th century, is also considered to be one of the finest works of the early Decorated style.

Brussels, Belgium

The Cathedral, in the heart of Brussels, used to be the collegiate church of St Michael and St Gudula, which was started at the beginning of the 13th century on the orders of Henry I, Duke of Brabant. This coincided with the birth in the Netherlands of the Gothic style. The work took about 300 years to complete, and its architecture shows the many varied characteristics of the Brabantine Gothic style. The restoration of the nave from 1983 to 1989 returned the stones,

Left: *the Cathedral of St Michael and St Gudula, Brussels*

vaults and windows to their former splendour. At the same time, important and well preserved remnants of the Romanesque church of the 11th century, over which the present Gothic church is built, were uncovered.

Since 1990, the nave has been closed for restoration, and it is hoped that the work will be completed soon, so that all visitors can again appreciate the fine pulpit carved by H F Verbruggen in 1699, that shows the Fall of Adam and Eve, and the Redemption as symbolised by the Immaculate Conception and the Infant Jesus carrying the cross.

The side aisles have stained glass from the 19th century and some 18th century confessional boxes in oak. On the altar of the first chapel on the northern side is a statue dating from 1592, of Our Lady of Deliverance.

The stained glass windows in the northern and southern transepts are by Jean Haeck, and were made from 1537 to 1538. Another stained glass window in the west front, inspired by the Renaissance and dating from 1528, depicts the Last Judgment. This is really best appreciated when standing immediately in front of the altar but with your back to it.

A bronze plaque affixed to the north wall of the Chapel of the Blessed Sacrament of the Miracle offers an explanation of events which took place in May 1370, but the story is too long to be fully detailed here, although in 1968 a formal declaration was then made by the authorities of the Archdiocese of Brussels Malines. There was an alleged theft by Jews of consecrated hosts, which were said to have bled at the time of their defilement. These events are well represented throughout the works of art in the Cathedral.

Burgos, Spain

The Cathedral of Santa María has many spires and stands on a granite hillside, overlooking the ancient town of Burgos, the former capital of Castile and the birthplace of *El Cid*. Begun in 1222, it is perhaps the most interesting of all of Spain's major Gothic cathedrals, and although not completed until the central lantern was put in place in 1568, the lapse of time has not lessened the stylistic unity of the many towers and pinnacles. In part, this is a result of the three generations of

the architects, the grand-
father, father and son, of the
Colenia family, who created
the unforgettable effect of
three groups of pale yellow
spires which force their way up
into a solid blue sky. Inside, the
dome of Burgos' crossing shows
that Moorish influences were
still affecting Spanish architecture as late as the middle of
the 16th century. It rises 50m
(164ft) above the floor of the
cathedral's nave.

Unfortunately the nave is
narrow, and the immense rebuilt crossing piers are clumsy
and awkward. Burgos is, however, rich in chapels, none
being more impressive than the
octagonal Connétable Chapel,
which is adorned with a vast
profusion of sculptures in the
Isabelline style, and includes a
single figure of St James and a
Visitation group. The Chapel of
St Nicholas has an unusually
ornate double stairway, built in
1519, with a metal balustrade; it
bears the arms of Bishop
Fonseca. Other monuments
and works of art abound, and
for the visitor *El Cid*'s tomb,
the storied cloisters and an
old chapterhouse should not
be missed.

**Left: *Burgos, the Cathedral as
seen from the south west***

Canterbury, England

The mother church of the
Anglican faith, Canterbury is
the diocese of the Archbishop
of Canterbury, Primate of All
England. Built between 1070
and 1505, it is essentially the
work of separated centuries as
little work was carried out for
200 years, between 1180 and 1380.
Its styles are Perpendicular,
west of the central tower, and
early Gothic over a Norman
crypt at the east end. It is the
fourth longest of English
cathedrals, measuring 156m
(512ft), but in area only the
ninth.

An original Saxon cathedral
existed on the current site and
was burnt down in 1067. The
Norman cathedral was begun
by Lanfranc, the first Archbishop under William the
Conqueror in about 1070. This
replacement cathedral was
considered to be too small,
however, and in 1096 Archbishop Anselm, who was
Lanfranc's successor, began to
rebuild the east end. This work
was expanded by Prior Conrad,
and although the work was
completed in 1130, his efforts
were destroyed by the fire in
1174, which left only the outer
aisle walls standing.

By then, the act that dominates the history of Canterbury

had already taken place, when on 29 December 1170 at King Henry II's instigation Archbishop Thomas Becket was murdered in his own cathedral. Becket was canonised in 1193, since when Canterbury has been a place of pilgrimage. Today over 2.3 million visitors travel to the Cathedral every year.

The rebuilding began in 1175, directed by the French master mason William of Sens, who completed the east transept. He then handed over to William the Englishman, who completed the St Thomas chapel, Becket's Crown and the crypt below. It was then a further 200 years before Lanfranc's nave was demolished to make way for the magnificent spacious nave that now replaces it. This

Canterbury, Mother Church of the Anglican faith

was built by Henry Yevele in between 1391 and 1405. The old north east tower was replaced in 1834 with a copy of the south west tower, which had been built from 1424 to 1434.

On entering the Cathedral by the west front, the nave appears well lit, probably because of the loss of the original stained glass. To the left, and under the north west tower, is a memorial to the Archbishop Benson, and near to it is the Corinthian Throne. The ornate font is in the second bay of the north aisle. From this position in the nave, there is an excellent view of the 15th century screen that separates the nave from the choir. The screen, which has its original iron gates, shows the crowned figures of Henry V, Richard II, Ethelbert, Edward the Confessor, Henry IV and Henry VI.

The north east transept, known as the Martyrdom, was where Becket was murdered, the four knights entering from the cloisters through a door. A stone slab now marks the spot, said to replace a bloodstained section of the original floor which was cut out and sent as a relic to Rome. It is also marked with another slab, recalling that the Pope, John Paul II, and Archbishop Robert Runcie knelt together to pray on 29 May 1982.

There are many tombs within Canterbury, including at the east end the stone coffin of Archbishop Stephen Langton, who helped the barons to persuade King John to sign *Magna Carta* in 1215. Between the south piers is that of Edward, the Black Prince, (*d* 1376), together with reproductions of his armour; the originals may be seen in a case in the south choir aisle.

The marble chair known as St Augustine's Chair is the one on which the Primates of All England are enthroned, and is situated behind the High Altar.

Also behind the High Altar and Chair, the Trinity Chapel, built in honour of St Thomas, is reached by steps. Until 1538 it contained his elaborate shrine, which could be viewed by pilgrims through a grille, the site now being marked by a much worn pavement.

Calahorra, Spain

The cathedral of Calahorra and that of Santo Domingo de la Calzada share one diocese, and although Calahorra now gives no impression of a cathedral city, this little market town set on a hill is much larger than the simple country town that is Santo Domingo de la Calzada, where the Cathedral dominates the entire landscape, with one of the finest spires in all Spain.

At Calahorra, the smallish cathedral, only 72m (236ft) long, was begun in 1485. It boasts an impressive early Renaissance north door, with a multitude of small figures. The great arch is framed between Ionic attached columns, standing upon the lower order of fine Corinthian pilasters flanking the doors; the spandrels above the arch contain large figures of angels in low relief. The building of the Cathedral was finished in 1704, when the west front and tower were completed.

Chartres, France

This marvellous Cathedral was built in just a quarter of a century, whereas ordinarily the construction of a cathedral was a matter of many decades or even centuries. Even the great churches had tended to become kaleidoscopes of architectural styles as successive masons and architects died or were supplanted by others, each in turn being anxious to express his own concepts and to leave his mark upon posterity.

Owing to the collective zeal

The easily recognisable west front of Chartres Cathedral now looks down on excavation works

of its citizens, Chartres is the purest example of the ogival style ever constructed, and marks a watershed in Gothic architecture, with simplicity of construction, beauty of form, and strong workmanship in a judicious choice of materials. As with many other cathedrals, Chartres stands on the site of a previous church; however, in this case, there had been five previous churches, all of which had burnt down with the exception of the fifth; of which, when it fell victim in 1194, the crypt, towers and Royal Portal were saved, and even now survive. Extensive excavation work in front of the west front has uncovered some Roman remains, which are still being examined.

The present Cathedral was dedicated in 1260, following the rebuilding which had begun in 1230. It measures 130.02m (426ft 7in) in length with a 16.4m (53ft 9in) wide nave. The height of the vault is 37.5m (123ft), that of the south tower and steeple 103m (337ft 11in), and of the north tower and steeple 112m (367ft 6in).

Chartres Cathedral stands majestically above all of the surrounding buildings, a clear symbol for all to see, but to stand inside at the crossing of the transept and the nave and to behold the three rose windows is a humbling and awesome experience.

Chester, England

Following the rebuilding of Chester in 907 by Ethelfleda, daughter of King Alfred and wife of Ethelred, a church was built on the site of the present Cathedral. In 1092 it was turned into a Benedictine abbey by Hugh Lupus, nephew of William the Conqueror. The present Cathedral, which incorporates the remains of the Norman abbey on the north side, was begun in 1250 and reflects successive building periods up to the 19th century.

The Lady Chapel dates from 1250, the choir from *c* 1300, and the arcades of the south transept and the south arcade of the nave from the middle of the 14th century. The remainder of the nave, the clerestory of the south transept and the top stages of the tower date from the end of the 15th century. The south front of the south transept was begun in 1819 and a major restoration was begun in

1868 by Sir George Gilbert Scott, architect of the Grand Hotel at St Pancras Station, London. This affected much of both the exterior and the interior, including the turrets on the central tower and the west front. Even the west front itself, in spite of its very fine Perpendicular window, adds to this conflation of styles.

Internally the Cathedral is uncluttered and the warm red of the stone generates a sense of security. The mosaics that cover the wall of the north aisle and illustrate biblical scenes were added by J R Clayton, in 1886.

The chapter house contains the Cathedral's finest stained glass, showing St Werburgh's history, and the wood carving on the choir stalls of the 15th century is widely considered the best of its type in England.

Coutances, France

The Cathedral of Nôtre Dame at Coutances has a simple feeling of well being about it. There are neither any overpowering nor any excessively impressive embellishments to distract from the integrity of line and proportion of this most nearly perfect of all of the Norman cathedrals.

Situated on an outcrop on the banks of the River Soulles, it was begun in 1048 and is the work of Geoffroy de Montbray, the Bishop of Coutances, who later served under William the Conqueror as a warrior priest in England. He had inherited an existing cathedral much in

Chester frater pulpit, one of the best of three remaining in England, from which the lector would read to the monks during meals

The east end (apse) of Coutances, with the lantern tower clearly visible and the Lady Chapel in the foreground

need of repair, and set about raising funds to rebuild it. His cathedral was consecrated in 1056 with William present.

In 1210, Bishop Hugues de Morville started to build the present Cathedral, which was completed in 1274, and which has remained basically the same ever since. It embodies much of the earlier building, and includes its central lantern tower, with which Geoffroy de Montbray had crowned his church and which rises 58m (190ft) above the floor of the nave. Undoubtedly this is one of the very finest to be seen anywhere.

45

Durham, England

Standing on a bold peninsula, almost surrounded by the river Wear, Durham holds the most dramatic city site in England, with the great Norman Cathedral on the summit of a wooded bank that rises abruptly from the river. This may perhaps be best appreciated when viewed from the railway.

A monastery was founded in 995 on the current site, and this gave way to the Cathedral that was begun by Bishop William de St Carileph in 1093, who completed the choir and the crossing. The church was designed to be vaulted, and the ribbed vault of the north choir aisle is possibly the oldest in England. The Norman choir originally ended in an apse, but underwent alterations in the late 13th century, and now terminates in the Chapel of the Nine Altars.

The Cathedral's interior is solemn, with its alternating square and circular piers incised and decorated by the remarkable patterned carving and zigzag mouldings. In the pavement east of the font is a line of black Frosterley marble, beyond which no woman was allowed to pass, in accordance with Benedictine rule; the font itself is a small Renaissance period piece and surrounded by a towering tabernacle.

The many pillared galilee Chapel is entered from the west end of the nave. It contains the simple 16th century tomb of the Venerable Bede, who died at Jarrow in 735. His remains were brought to Durham in 1020, before being placed to rest in the galilee in 1370.

The choir is separated from the crossing by a light, open screen of differently coloured marble which replaces an earlier wooden screen.

Ely, England

A Benedictine abbey had been founded at Ely in 673 by Queen Etheldreda of Northumbria. By the time the Normans reached Ely, the abbey had been both rebuilt and reconsecrated by Ethelwold, to become one of England's greatest religious centres. After the Conquest a former Prior of Winchester, Simeon, was appointed abbot, and he set about enlarging the existing church, beginning work in 1083. The transepts and east end were finished by 1106, three years after the elevation of the church to cathedral rank. The immense Norman nave was finished in 1189, and at the very end of the century, the galilee had been completed.

In the second quarter of the 13th century, Bishop Hugh of Northwold added extensively to the choir by installing six magnificent new bays, which were unfortunately destroyed in 1322 when the Cathedral's central tower toppled into them.

This apparent disaster led to Ely's glory, when the architect Alan of Walsingham and the master carpenter William Hurle constructed a unique central octagon which was to be capped with the only Gothic dome there is. This takes the form of an octagonal wooden lantern that was so set that the angles are juxtaposed with the faces of the immense octagon that supports it *see page 18*.

The choir is separated from the octagon by a 19th century screen, and the narrow nave, which consists of 12 bays, is nearly 76.2m (250ft) long. As well as being one of the most varied, Ely is also one of the longest English cathedrals, at 157.5m (517ft), yet it stands less than 21.3m (70ft) high.

Evreux, France

A cathedral at Evreux is first mentioned in 912; consecrated in 1076, it was burnt down by Henry I of England in 1119. In between 1123 and 1140 the Cathedral was restructured, and the great Romanesque arches that can be seen today in the nave date from this time. The Cathedral again fell victim to the torch in 1194, courtesy of Philip II. However, although the damage was not nearly so extensive as on the previous occasion, it did result in the higher parts of the nave having to be rebuilt, and this, together

The Lady Chapel at Evreaux, France

with work on the triforium, clerestory and vaults, was all completed in 1253. The choir was reconstructed between 1270 and 1310.

Although the fire of 1356 did little damage, since then there has been one further major fire, caused by German bombing in 1940, which severely damaged the western part. A hail storm in August 1983 destroyed many of the 14th century stained glass windows for which Evreux was famous. These are now under restoration. However, the best remained undamaged, including those which have the Virgin as their theme and form the windows to the choir. The choir itself, conceived in the classical Gothic style and surrounded by 13 chapels, is certainly outstanding.

Evreux measures 108.87m (357ft 2in) in length, the nave is 25.42m (83ft 5in) wide and 21.75m (71ft 4in) high, while the spire attains 75m (246ft) after its rebuilding since the last War.

Ferrara, Italy

The large Cathedral of San Giorgio was consecrated in 1135, and features some Gothic elements in arches of the upper façade, and in the loggia over

The south aisle wall of Ferrara Cathedral, with its double thickness of blind arches and the occasional small window

the central door. Three peaked gables of equal size and height dominate the façade, where the sculptures of the main portal are attributed to Niccolò, a 12th century artist. The dark interior contains a plethora of candelabra, both down and across the nave, which are made necessary by the double layered blind arches along the length of the aisles. Outside the south wall runs a two storey arcade, with chic boutiques at street level and living apartments above.

Left: *the west front of Our Lady of Evreux, which is one of the most beautiful examples of religious architecture in Normandy*

Florence, Italy

At the end of the 13th century there was a time of peace and also of immense creativity in Florence. The city fathers, not to be outdone by the ambitions of Pisa and Siena where cathedral projects were underway, proclaimed their desire for 'an edifice ... so magnificent ... that it shall surpass anything of the kind produced in the time of their greatest power by the Greeks and Romans'. The site chosen for the new Cathedral was the one occupied by the very ancient church of Santa Reparata, and the foundation

for the new church was blessed in 1296, under the aegis of Pope Boniface VIII.

An impressive beginning was made to the nave, with two aisles each with four bays, terminating in an octagon with side chapels. However, progress was then slow, with the plans being frequently altered amid constant controversy. Finally the nave was completed in 1420, and the chapels surrounding the octagon were all roofed.

The drum had been put up, ready for the cupola which was to be 42.7m (140ft) in diameter, but there was not an architect in Italy who had the remotest notion of just how to construct the Cathedral's crowning glory, which was to be much bigger than anything hitherto attempted. A competition was held, after which Filippo Brunelleschi was able to convince the building commission of the feasibility of his plan to buttress the octagonal substructure of the crossing with a series of half-domed apse chapels, thereby creating a kind of external skeleton of eight graceful curving ribs. His majestic dome, which made all subsequent domes in Europe possible, was indeed built 'in a

Left: *the tympanum of the west portal of Florence Cathedral*

50

style of magnificence which neither the industry nor the power of man' has ever surpassed.

The cupola was painted with the Universal Judgement in fresco by Giorgio Vasari and Federigo Zuccari. This, along with a few memorial frescoes in the nave, the retables of the altars and in addition the unusually richly coloured glass of the chapel windows, are the only colour in the church. The few sculptures seem particularly fitting in this spatial environment, with the *Pietà* by Michelangelo in the left transept.

The vast extent of red, white and green marble encrusted walls, the white marble gables of the carved doorways, and the red roofs of the nave and cupola are deeply memorable. The imposing east end, with the complex pattern of the polygonal chapels buttressing it on every side, is firmly united to the nave by the elaborate cornices which run from end to end; the horizontal lines are relieved by the shallow buttresses, the arcading and the neutralising circles of the upper windows. However, it is all subordinated to the cupola, the firm curves of which rise high above to the white marble lantern with its ball and cross.

Frankfurt, Germany

The St Bartholomew Cathedral is one of the great historic buildings in Germany, for it was here, from the 14th century until 1792, that kings and emperors of Germany were crowned. This was the result of Charles IV's 'Golden Bull' issued in 1356.

The church is a 13th century Gothic structure, and is renowned for its choir frescoes of 1427, which depict the life of the Cathedral's patron saint, and its 94.2m (309ft) spired tower, with its Imperial 12.2 tonne (12 ton) bell, the *Gloriosa*.

Freiburg, Germany

Freiburg represents one of the most remarkable glories of German Gothic art. Its filigree spire is a slender 115.8m (380ft) shaft of petrified lace, designed by Master Remigius Faesch of Basel in the 14th century, and has since been the model for many other cathedrals along the Rhine, including the west spires of the great Cathedral at Köln.

The church, which was built between 1122 and 1252, has gained a large collection of precious works of art, that includes altar paintings by Hans Buldung Gruen, panels by Lucas Cranach the Elder and Hans Holbein the Younger. There is much fine sculpture of French influence adorning the portals, especially that of St Nicholas' Chapel, and corbels. There is also a celebrated bell, known as *Hosanna*. This is one of the oldest in Germany, and weighs in at 5.1 tonnes (5 tons).

Genoa, Italy

The influence of French Gothic architecture reached Genoa owing to its close proximity to France quite early in the 14th century, when work on the restoration of the 11th century Cathedral of San Lorenzo was undertaken. A Renaissance dome surmounts the Gothic façade. The choir, by contrast, is early Genoese Baroque, but these quite disparate elements of the Cathedral make a rather surprising and harmonious whole. The relics of St John the Baptist are contained in a much ornamented chapel.

Gerona, Spain

Gerona is famous for the immense vault of its aisleless nave; the notion of applying the solution of a single span can be credited to Jacques Favran, who had been the architect of St Jean at Perpignan, and first proposed the idea for Gerona. It was, however, a hundred years before his ideas were finally promulgated by Guillem Bofill. Following his appointment as architect in 1415, the latter had persuaded a conference of architects to accept the idea, and the single span nave was built. It is still today the widest Gothic vault in existence, at 22.5m (74ft).

Gerona possesses an early tower, known as the Tower of Charlemagne, on the north side, built from 1038 to 1117, and a Romanesque cloister of about 1180 to 1210, although most of the Cathedral's construction was accomplished between the early 14th and late 16th centuries.

The cloister has carvings of various strange grotesques, while the tower has a singular system of decorative treatment, taking the form of six stages of blind recesses, each being capped by a series of small arches with round heads.

The Cathedral also possesses a marvellous silver altarpiece and canopy of the 14th century, which although damaged in the Civil War has been restored now. There is, too, a stone bishop's throne from the same period, beautifully simple in its design, and located in the choir. One further testimony to the adventurous undertakings of the architects of Gerona is the unique flying buttress of the chevet.

Ghent, Belgium

The simple structure of St Bavo's Cathedral, Ghent, is nevertheless impressive, and fully illustrates the development of Gothic architecture in Belgium. The choir shows how Scheldt Gothic was connected with northern French Gothic; the tower thus represents the Brabantine high Gothic and the nave points to the late Gothic style.

The Cathedral furniture still dates mostly from the 17th and 18th centuries, thanks mainly to the generosity of Bishop Antonius Triest; many works bear his coat of arms. However, most of the stained glass windows are dated after 1861. Those of the 15th and 16th centuries were almost destroyed by the iconoclasts, except for some fragments that can be seen in the second chapel along the north aisle from the west front.

The conventional layout has been shortened by bringing the altar forward, which partly covers the staircase in the transept leading to the choir. On each side of the chancel steps are life sized statues of SS Peter and Paul, carved in white marble. Also of note are the magnificent bronze cross and candlesticks of the 19th century, which were paid for by Napoleon I when he visited Ghent in 1803.

On each side of the High Altar are the magnificent mausoleums of some of the Bishops of Ghent, including that of Bishop Antonius Triest, a marble mausoleum carved by Jerome du Quesnoy the Younger, in which the Bishop is portrayed kneeling on the sarcophagus in his *cappa magna* and conversing with Death in the form of a skeleton in brass.

In the Villachapel, to the right of the west portal, is preserved one of the most famous masterpieces of all time, *The Adoration of the Mystic Lamb* by the brothers Hubert and Jan van Eyck, of 1432. A small fee is now being charged for entry into this chapel, but the magnificence of the work is more than worth it.

The crypt of St Bavo's is the largest and most remarkable in

Left: *the central panel from* The *Adoration of the Mystic Lamb at Ghent*

Belgium, undervaulting the whole area of the sanctuary. At present it consists of a nave, an ambulatory and a series of side and radiating chapels. Its very oldest part dates from the 12th century, being part of St John's church, which was built about 1150.

Gloucester, England

Built on the site of a small Saxon monastery, this ornate Cathedral is largely a Norman work, with a most beautiful pinnacled tower. It was constructed between 1089 and 1100 under the direction of Abbot Serlo, and dedicated in 1100.

It was not elevated to cathedral status until after the Dissolution in 1540, yet in 1216 the nine year old Henry III was crowned there and in 1327 the body of Edward II, who had been murdered at Berkeley Castle, was denied burial at Bristol and Malmesbury but was enshrined at Gloucester. After his death, his shrine became a focus of miracles and pilgrimage. The vast revenue thus accrued enabled the monks to hire a court mason and to rebuild in the new Perpendicular style, of which Gloucester became the first successful example in England.

The circular piers in the interior are massive, as well as exceptionally high; the 14th century choir is an excellent example of pure Perpendicular style unparalleled in England by virtue of the combination of its tracery, panelled walls, richly carved stalls, elaborate vaulting and the large east window which is the largest in the country, being 24.4m (80ft) high by 11.5m (38ft) wide.

From floor to ceiling, the design of the choir and transepts is a perfect unity and there are noteworthy tombs in the choir, including the very beautiful canopied tomb of Edward II. The choir triforium, with its barrel vault, is reached from the north transept. In 1981, as part of the 1,300th anniversary celebrations, the triforium was laid out as an exhibition permanently illustrating two parts of the Cathedral's history. To the north is shown the abbey period, and to the south the cathedral period from 1540 to the present. These two halves are linked by the Whispering Gallery, which runs outside the great east window and across the west end of the Lady Chapel.

Left, main picture: *an external view of Gloucester Cathedral; inset, the unusual lavatorium of the cloisters gives a hint of the beautiful fan vaulting that adorns this cathedral*

The central tower, 68.5m (225ft) high, commands extensive views across the Severn estuary. In the lower part hangs the only medieval great bell remaining in England, *Great Peter*, of 1420.

Köln, Germany

The Cathedral at Köln is huge; it is indeed the largest Gothic cathedral in northern Europe, and although it took many centuries to build, it is now the mother of all German cathedrals, the symbol of the city of Köln and the entire Rhineland.

In 1162, the Prussian Emperor Frederick I stormed Milan and 'liberated' the relics of the Three Magi from the bell tower of a Milan church, where they had rested for eight centuries after being sent there from Constantinople by Constantine the Great. These relics were delivered to Köln Cathedral, which had been built in the fourth century.

Archbishop Conrad decided in the 13th century that the relics needed an appropriately imposing shrine to house them and when the ancient and crumbling Cathedral caught fire it was left to burn itself out.

Master Gerard was charged with the job of drawing up plans for the new Cathedral, and he immediately began work on a chancel in a distinctly French Gothic style. The chancel, which rose 45.7m (150ft) into the air and is clearly reminiscent of that at Amiens where Gerard had previously worked, was consecrated in 1322. The overall plans, however, were dauntingly ambitious, and although the south tower came near to completion, once the bell had been hung there in 1437 work slowed markedly, and came to a halt in 1560, fortunately not until after some beautiful stained glass had been added.

It was another 282 years before work resumed. In 1842, after lost plans covering the unbuilt main towers, transepts, nave and west spires of the construction had been recovered in Darmstadt, King Frederick William IV decreed that the Cathedral would be completed as had been originally conceived. The work was completed in 1880, after completion of the towers with four storeys and elegant spires.

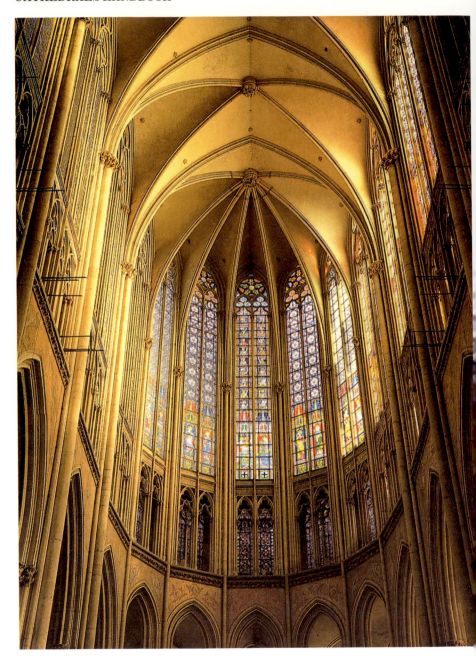

Previous pages, left: *the Three Magi windows in the High Chancel of Köln Cathedral; and* right, *the exceptional flying buttresses of Le Mans Cathedral, viewed from below the apse*

Le Mans, France

The Cathedral of St Julien at Le Mans can be considered as one of the most daring structures of the Middle Ages by virtue of its flying buttresses, which create the impression of carrying far more weight than they could possibly support.

Le Mans is one of the most inconsistent and confusing of medieval churches, its Gothic transept having replaced a Romanesque predecessor; yet the former now seems pinched and too narrow for its height. The nave is sombre, yet gives way to a brighter and more airy choir. Le Mans, like Evreux, suffered from fire, the Romanesque building having been burnt in the 11th century, and this was followed by another fire in 1134 at the same time as the fire at Chartres. It also suffered at the hands of the Huguenots during the religious conflicts of the 16th century, when they continued their destructive tradition, smashing everything within the church.

León, Spain

Famous for its nearly perfectly preserved original stained glass, León rates among the most important of Gothic art monuments. Its appearance is not typically Spanish, as it belongs more to the epoch of metropolitan French tradition in design. The building work, which began in 1255 on the chevet, spanned almost three centuries and was later to be influenced by Romanesque classicism, but the wide front and external towers with their narrow lancets flanking wider openings are repeated from 13th century English work.

The main influence however is however unmistakeably Reims, and the architect undoubtedly Enrique, who had charge of the work at Burgos; as at Burgos, Enrique was succeeded by Juan Pérez.

Internally, León is exquisite, with an elegance provided by the windows, which occupy a very large percentage of the wall space. There is a quite remarkable openwork triforium, architecturally linked to the clerestory, which is itself glazed. Much of León's famous glass is modern, having been

Right: *the south front of León Cathedral*

inserted during the great restoration at the end of the 19th century, but it was exceptionally well harmonised and is hard to discern. Because so much of the original glass had survived, the re-creation of the whole provides, as nowhere else perhaps in the world, a glowing atmosphere of light that was the ideal of all Gothic churches in northern Europe; indeed, the glass at León deserves a book to itself.

Lérida, Spain

The *Seu Vella* (Old Cathedral) of Lérida stands on a fortified promontory above the banks of the River Segre, built at the start of the 13th century. It is now surrounded by a modern town on the lower ground. It has been carefully restored, after 250 years as a barracks, to a gem of Transitional as well as Gothic art.

The strangely placed cloister serves as a forecourt, and is entered through a porch, the splendid Puerta de los Apóstoles. Through to the right, or south west angle of the cloister, is the octagonal belfry, while to the west the cloister is reinforced by massive buttresses. To the south there is a great traceried window, beyond which is an exceptional view of the plains, the Llanos de Urgel. Beyond the cloister, through the south door, is the entrance to the Cathedral nave, a round arched Romanesque construction that shelters behind the outer portico.

The work at Lérida was begun in 1203 by Pedro Decumbo. The Cathedral measures 85m (279ft) long, 47m (154ft) wide and the nave has a span of 11.5m (38ft). It contains a rich abundance of fine carvings and the remains of a wall painting of about 1300, in the sanctuary, depicting in line form scenes from the New Testament.

There is also a new Cathedral in Lérida, situated in the lower town. It was designed in 1760 by Pedro Mártir Cermeño, and as such is the only one in Spain to have been designed during the second half of the 18th century. Furthermore, it was the source of Morató's design for the rebuilt Cathedral at Vich, which lies 67km (41 miles) north of Barcelona. However, the new Cathedral at Lérida is both unexciting and unimpressive; all of the fittings were destroyed in 1936, when the church was both sacked and fired, although the structural damage has since been repaired, it remains a poor monument.

London (St Paul's), England

In 1666, the existing cathedral was practically burned down in the Great Fire of London, and Wren was instructed to design its successor. He then produced plans for an entirely new cathedral, and building was begun in 1675. In 1697, the first service was held in the choir and the last stone was put in place in 1708, the entire building being completed during Wren's lifetime. He now lies buried in the building's crypt, his epitaph engraved above the entrance: *Si monumentum requiris, circumspice* (If you want a monument, look around you).

St Paul's stood unaltered until 1941 when, during German air attacks on London, the building received two direct hits from high explosive bombs.

The famous dome of St Paul's lifts its cross 111.25m (365ft), symbolically one foot for each day of the year. The outer dome was constructed in the same style as St Peter's, Rome, with a double skin, the outer dome being of wood covered with lead. The weight of the lantern on the top is borne by a cone of brick rising between an inner brick dome and the outer dome.

Inside, St Paul's follows the usual plan of a Gothic church; it has a nave and aisles with triforium and clerestory transepts and choir with the great dome space at the crossing.

The inner cupola of the dome, which is 66.4m (218ft) above the floor level rests on 12 massive supports. In the spandrels of the dome are mosaics which were added at the same time as those in the choir, of 1863-97, by Antonio Salviati of Venice. The paintings in the dome were completed earlier in 1720 by Sir James Thornhill and depict in eight scenes the life of St Paul.

Behind the High Altar is the Jesus Chapel, which occupies the eastern apse of the Cathedral. It is the memorial to America's fallen in the Second World War, with a roll of honour containing the names of 28,000 Americans who died in operations based on Britain. A replica book can be consulted by relatives on application to a verger.

The crypt corresponds in size with the upper church, and has now been fully restored since the damage of 50 years ago. It includes a new Treasury and an audio visual lecture room and houses Wren's Great Model of the Cathedral, which is 6.1m (20ft) long, made of oak, and which took nine months to make between 1673 and 1674.

Most of the original building costs of about £750,000 were

An outstanding example of Baroque; the dome of St Paul's Cathedral, London, at night inset; and **main picture** *the dome contains the eight paintings by James Thornhill*

raised by a tax on coal coming in to London by sea.

Lucca, Italy

The Cathedral of San Martino was founded on the site of a sixth century church by Bishop Anselmo Badagio, who was later to become Pope Alexander II. Major rebuilding in the 14th century did away with all of Badagio's Romanesque structure, except for the original choir, apse and aisles. Lucca's impressive façade was begun some time after 1204 by the architect Guidetto da Como and several Lombard sculptors, who also created a relief group depicting the Cathedral's patron, St Martin, with the beggar. Although Lucca's façade is closely patterned on that of Pisa, it is notable in its own right for its rich embellishment, its intricacy of detail, and its inlaid marble of various colours, among which a deep green predominates.

Like its exterior, Lucca's three aisled interior successfully combines subtle colour harmony with lavish ornamentation. A solid gold candelabrum hangs above the entrance to the *Tempieto*, the Cathedral's octagonal chapel. The Cathedral's most sacred treasure, however, is *Il Volto Santo* (Holy Face). This is a wooden crucifix with a robed figure of Christ, which as the story relates was carved by St Nicodemus, finished by an angel, and then conveyed in a boat with no crew from Palestine to Italy and thence to Lucca in a chariot drawn by wild bulls.

Il volto Santo **is kept in a little Renaissance temple which is located half way down the left aisle of San Martino**

Our Lady of Almudena, Madrid, as seen from the narrow streets of San Justo

Madrid, Spain

Madrid is another Spanish city with two cathedrals, neither of which is inspiring. The older of the two is the *colegiata* of San Isidro el Real, which was built between 1622 and 1664 as the church of the Jesuits. Although its structural damage has been put right, again its internal glories departed in 1936, when it was sacked.

The new Cathedral of Nuestra Señora de la Almudena was begun in 1880, and although it remains unfinished, it is far more impressive than the other, with a neo Romanesque crypt and solid columns, and parts of the arcade in neo Gothic.

Milan, Italy

The Cathedral of Milan is the greatest Italian architectural project of the late 14th century and, with the exception of Seville, is the largest medieval cathedral in Europe. The fabric of this remarkable building is of brick, with facings and window mullions of pinkish marble from Candoglia, where quarries owned in perpetuity by the Cathedral Chapter are still worked for all restoration

Above: *the marble spires which grace Milan Cathedral are all topped by statues*

purposes. The overwhelming complexity and detail of the ornamentation of the exterior defy close description, yet conform to the regular structural pattern, with which they are integrated. The serried ranks of pinnacled and canopied buttresses on the massive plinth

Left: *detail of a stained glass window behind the altar, Milan Cathedral*

around the main walls, the labyrinth of pinnacled fretted flying buttresses above the high aisles and the slender perforated spire shooting up from the lantern all give brilliant movement to the colossal body of the building. The whole is decorated with no fewer than 2,245 sculpted figures.

The vast interior is lofty and austere, with plain surfaces to the walls and piers. The clear uniformity of the design was determined when the ambulatory and choir, the principal structural components for the east end, had been built. The tall piers, with eight slender attached shafts, rise up to the springing of the vaults in the aisle and nave, but the unique capitals set below the level of the inner aisle vault dominate and weigh down their vertical lines. The prolonged labour in completing so grandiose a building lasted nearly 500 years.

Nantes, France

On 28 January 1972, a fire nearly destroyed the entire Cathedral at Nantes, which had been begun in April 1434 by special request of Duke John V by Guillaume de Dammartin. As a consequence of that fire, the Ministry of Culture and Historic Monuments decided to restore the Cathedral, and on 13 May 1985 Bishop Marcus of Nantes had the pleasure of inaugurating the renovated Cathedral during a concert of sacred music. On 2 June this was followed by a solemn mass attended by 4,000 worshippers. This is the only cathedral in France to have a completely restored interior, which is most beautifully renovated.

Originally the Cathedral had taken nearly 50 years to build, and in 1577 the inauguration of the nave and aisles took place. The southern transept was completed about 1650, the northern transept was started in 1840, and after this the construction of the central transept, the choir and its five apsidal chapels followed almost without interruption for 51 years. It was on 25 December 1891, 450 years after the laying

Overleaf, left: *the Holy Virgin Chapel at Nantes, with stained glass windows by J le Moal; and* **right** *the west front of Nantes, with the portals of St Peter (right), and St Paul (left)*

of the first stone, that Bishop Lecoq inaugurated the entirely completed Cathedral.

Flamboyant Gothic in style, the Cathedral has purity of line and a deep nave which has no capitals to break the line of the pillars. It contains the highest and largest stained glass window extant in France, by Francis Chappuis. This represents on seven levels the bishops of Nantes, the saints, the martyrs and the blessed of Brittany. The polychrome marble High Altar dates from 1750, and the choir organ, one of the most important of its kind in France, has 31 stops. The Grand Organ is one of the most renowned in France, being composed of more than 6,000 pipes and 74 stops.

Norwich, England

One of the most majestic of all English cathedrals, Norwich has retained its Norman plan and structure almost completely, being 140.5m (461ft) long and with a soaring spire 96m (315ft) high, which is the second tallest in the country after Salisbury.

Begun by Bishop Herbert de Losinga in 1096, it was dedicated in 1101 but not completed until 1499. The Cathedral was burnt in 1272 when the townspeople revolted against the clergy. It was repaired after the Restoration in 1660, and the new east chapel was added in between 1930 and 1932 on part of the site of the 13th century Lady Chapel. This plainest of buildings has most beautiful flying buttresses, and the interior is equally plain and is unadorned with monuments.

The Bishop's Throne, behind the altar, is of the greatest interest, as taken with its surroundings it preserves the plan of the Christian sanctuary normal until about 1100. This plan probably dates back to the beginnings of Christianity and may have been derived from the Roman law courts, with the judge sitting on a throne in the centre of the apse with officials ranged around it on each side of him. The chair itself is eighth century or earlier, and may have come originally from Dunwich's Saxon cathedral. There are also remarkable cloisters, the only two storeyed monastic cloister in England. They were originally built in the 12th century, rebuilt in between 1300 and 1430, and restored between 1935 and 1938.

Right: *the majestic spire of Norwich Cathedral*

Orléans, France

Begun in 1287 by Bishop Gilles de Patay on the burnt out site of an earlier Romanesque church, it had not been completed before being demolished by the Huguenots in 1568, who left only some exterior walls and the apse chapels standing. Rebuilding was begun in 1601 by Henry IV, following the original Gothic plans.

The façade, with its two spireless towers, five portals surmounted by three rose windows and an open gallery, was rebuilt in 1759 by Louis XV's architect Gabriel.

Inside the life of the city's patron saint, Joan of Arc, is shown by Jacques Galland in a series of stained glass windows. The choir stalls, that are dated between 1702 and 1706, are particularly beautiful.

main part of the Cathedral is a Romanesque structure with nascent Gothic features such as the bases and heavy carved circular capitals of the nave columns. The pavement of the nave is all pink marble, and its only adornment is a set of 20 inlaid concentric octagons, each containing a single *fleur de lys*.

The choir stalls are among the most precious of their kind. They were begun in 1329, and contain relief figures carved underneath the canopies of the stalls, together with fine inlaid patterns and images of saints. The walls of the north chapel of the transept are inlaid with marble mosaic and the Chapel of the Madonna di San Brizio in the south transept was largely decorated, from 1408 onwards, with the celebrated frescoes by both Fra Angelico and Luca Signorelli.

Orvieto, Italy

This architectural gem, one of the most satisfying of medieval Tuscan monuments, stands on its podium regularly bounded on every side by courses not only of basalt but travertine, dominating the surrounding plain. Building work was not begun until about 1290; the

Osma, Spain

Dominating the whole city and the surrounding area as far as the eye can see, the Cathedral of Burgo de Osma is of the purest Gothic with the single exception of the tower. This was not begun until 1739, and is one of the finest products of Spanish Baroque. The church was begun in 1232, and is on a large scale, being 108m (354ft) in length and 50m (164ft) wide, the nave spanning 11.9m (39 ft) and a height of 20m (66ft), with the tower reaching 72m (236ft).

The plan follows that of Cuenca, but the construction was influenced by the Cathedral at Burgos. The beauty and grace of the statuary in the porch are quite remarkable, as is the tomb made for the local saint, San Pedro de Osma, which is situated in the north transept. This was made in 1258, and the effigy portrays the saint with his head lying sideways upon a pillow being tilted up by angels. The sides of the tomb are amazingly carved, showing in high relief scenes from the saint's life, his miracles and his death, quite without any containing architectural framework.

Also worth visiting are the large cloisters and the vestry, a square chamber divided into nine bays of ribbed vaulting supported upon four slender columns. Above it, and reached from the transept by a double staircase, is the chapel of San Pedro, a Renaissance structure contrasting sharply with the style of the neighbouring cloisters.

Palencia, Spain

Known as *la Bella Desconocida* (ie the 'Beautiful Unknown') Palencia is not an outstanding cathedral, but it is pleasant as

The south side of Palencia Cathedral, from the Plaza de la Immaculada, with the cloisters on the left

well as large, being constructed in warm creamy stone and covered in part with a rich orange brown patina. It is laid out in the form of a Latin cross, with three naves. The foundation stone was laid on 1 June 1321, on top of the crypt, which is now entered through a barrel-vaulted apsidal chamber of the 11th century. This is all that remains of a basilica begun in 672, which itself had been constructed on the site of the primitive cave of martyr San Antoninus of the second century.

During the 16th century many important works of art found their way to the Cathedral, including two splendid altarpieces, one by a Dutch artist now displayed in the choir, the other by a Spaniard and in the main chapel. The other woodcarvings, statues, tapestries and paintings also include one of St Sebastian by El Greco. One of Palencia's more curious features is its clock, which is located high up in the south transept, where a knight and a lion strike the hours and the quarter hours.

The cloisters at Pamplona, where once again extensive building work is underway, though due to be completed during 1995

Pamplona, Spain

Here the Cathedral is a large complex, backing onto the ancient city wall. It was built during the 11th century, but by the end of the 14th century it had fallen into such disrepair that it took nearly 130 years to rebuild. The old Romanesque façade was finally replaced in between 1780 and 1783, by the architect Ventura Rodríguez, and now nothing remains of the original church.

The Cathedral is dedicated to Our Lady, and contains some fine sculpture, particularly the carvings over the doorways of the Gothic cloister, which is a haven of sunshine and calm. These celebrate the common theme of the cult of the Virgin; the death of Mary is illustrated over the door leading to the cloister, and inside the cloister there is a 14th century relief of the Adoration of the Magi.

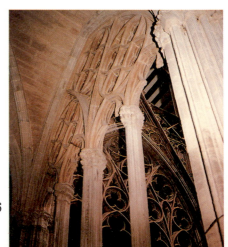

Paris (Nôtre Dame), France

Nôtre Dame stands on ground sacred to man since tribes of Celts first erected upon it their wood and reed tabernacles to pagan gods. Here too the all conquering Romans had built a temple to Jupiter. In the fourth century a Christian church stood here, and in the sixth century the walls of a basilica were built up around the earlier church, but the Nôtre Dame that we know today is the result of Bishop Maurice de Sully's plans for what was to become the first truly Gothic cathedral. For some 700 years this edifice has been the symbolic heart of Paris, with its buttresses rooted deep in the earth, and prevailing against the storms that have gathered and swirled about it.

The Bishop devoted his life to the project, having commissioned an unknown architect. He first raised funds, which enabled him to purchase a large number of houses, which he then pulled down. Through the rubble he drove a new road to the Cathedral site, over which he could transport the required building materials. The energetic Bishop also organised and ordered, purchased materials and selected the artists and left enough money in his will for the Cathedral roof to be covered with lead.

The construction crews took over the heart of the city, using the roofless ruin of the fourth century church of St Etienne situated alongside the new construction as their main work shop. The name of St Etienne is still commemorated in the name of the north door of the present Cathedral. Tents, work shops, dormitories, dining halls, foundries and kilns had rapidly sprung up all around to deal with the timber, sand and stone that began to fill not just the streets but the cloisters of the Merovingian basilica, which were soon going to be pulled down in order to make way for the nave, towers and main façade of the new Cathedral.

The first stone of the Cathedral proper was blessed by Pope Alexander III in the company of Bishop Sully and King Louis VII in 1163, when foundations in the choir were just ready to receive the walls and shafts. The choir, with the exception of the roof, double side aisles and galleries, was completed in 1182, when sculptors started work on the doorways in the façade. The High Altar was consecrated on 19 May 1196.

The second stage, from 1180 to 1200, saw the erection of the

Left: Nôtre Dame's south transept; its rose window, dating from 1270, is illustrated on the front cover and depicts the triumph of Christ, with scenes from the New Testament, and inset is an aerial view of the great Gothic cathedral

west wall and the west piers of the transepts, the last three double bays of the nave, with the bays of the two side aisles, the sanctuary, ambulatory and galleries. During the third stage, from 1190 to 1220, the two rectangular towers were begun, together with the linking bay of the nave, and also the west front was erected up to the level of the rose window, which was itself added between 1220 and 1225.

The final stage, between 1225 and 1240, saw the completion of both the south tower and the north tower with the high and lofty gallery between the two completed. Nôtre Dame was the first Gothic church to surpass Cluny; it is the last of the great galleried churches, of which Laón is a prime example. It was also the first to use flying buttresses and demonstrates the classically harmonious Gothic style at its best.

The interior between the towers is quite without precedent, comprised of a pre-nave just two bays deep, in front of the central nave which has two pairs of side aisles to align with three portals. The outer side aisles are flanked externally on each side by seven chapels, which continue around the choir and apse to total 27 in all.

The elevation is on three levels, and the galleries can hold 1,500 people. The vaulting is supported on 75 piers.

Parma, Italy

Parma's Santa María Assunta is the largest of the Lombard region Romanesque churches. Begun in 1038, the Cathedral was not consecrated until 1106 and remained unfinished until the middle of the 13th century. The great dome over the transept was painted by Antonio Allegri, known to posterity as Correggio, with an Assumption of the Virgin. This work caused much controversy at the time, as the figures all have much foreshortened torsoes; there is an apparent abundance of limbs.

The Baptistery, a separate building the work of Benedetto Antelami, dates from 1196. It contains three magnificently carved tympani, especially the splendid Portal of the Virgin. The 13th century bell tower completed the complex.

Peterborough, England

Founded in 656 by Penda, King of Mercia, as a Benedictine monastery, Peterborough was destroyed by the Danes in 870. Rebuilt in 971, it was sacked in 1116, with restoration beginning immediately afterwards. The interior was destroyed in 1643 by Puritans, but again later restored.

The ornate west front, composed of three enormous recessed arches, opens into a magnificent light Norman nave with finely vaulted aisles and a unique 13th century wooden painted ceiling. The triforium and clerestory are dignified, and the nave piers massive in appearance although they are hollow shells filled with rubble.

The sanctuary is the oldest part of the building. In the north choir aisle is a fine tomb slab of Abbot Benedict, who was responsible for the building of the nave. To the side is a stone memorial to Catherine of Aragon, beneath the banners of England and Spain. At the end of the south choir the Monk's Stone is a memorial to the monks of Peterborough who were killed by the Danes in 870. The original burial place of Mary, Queen of Scots (*d* 1587) is marked by a slab beneath a Scottish banner.

Pisa, Italy

A naval victory over Saracens at Palermo in 1063 resulted in a rich booty, which the citizens of Pisa then decided to use in part to erect a splendid temple worthy of the Divine Majesty. The Romanesque Cathedral in white marble was begun, and following another victory, this time over the city of Amalfi in 1153, the Pisans decided to celebrate with a circular marble baptistery. However funds ran out in 1278, and the work was suspended to be completed later by the architect and sculptor Nicola Pisano, who with the help of his son brought the building with its curved lead and tile covered dome to completion in a style that complemented that of the Cathedral.

The famous 'Leaning Tower', the campanile, was begun in 1172, but when the architects became aware that it was slightly out of plumb, work was stopped: in fact, the building had sunk 1.8m (6ft) into the ground on the south side. When work was resumed after a gap of 16 years, no attempt was made to correct this, but instead the weight of the upper storeys was distributed so as to maintain a precarious equilibrium, which has lasted to this day.

Pistoia, Italy

Famous for its solid silver altar of St James of the 13-14th centuries which portrays 628 figures in bas-relief, the Cathedral itself is mainly of the 12th century Pisan Romanesque style, with rows of small arches on the façades and a polychrome wooden framed nave.

When the altar was stolen in 1295, Dante consigned the thief to his *Inferno*; however the Cathedral also numbers among its many treasures the Gobelin tapestries which are behind the altar, a Virgin and Andrea della Robbia's superb terracotta group; there is also a Verrocchio funerary monument.

The porch and tympanum over the west front door of Pistoia

Prague, the Czech Republic

The original church of St Vitus was a rotunda, erected about 929 by Prince Wenceslas. On the site of the rotunda, between 1060 and 1096, a Romanesque basilica was built, consisting of a nave and single aisles.

In 1344, the Prague bishopric was raised to an archbishopric, and this led to the building of the Gothic Cathedral. The form follows that of the French cathedrals, with a ring of chapels round the choir and a complicated system to give support.

The Cathedral was plundered by the Calvinists in 1619, during the rebellion of the Estates, and was changed into a house of prayer. It was completed, as was the very essential repair work, by the Union in 1929, and the final church measures 124m (407ft) long by 60m (200ft) wide and 33m (108ft) high; the height of the principal tower is 99.6m (327ft).

Above the pillared arcade, the triforium runs round the whole Cathedral, the inner passage containing a gallery of 21 sculpted portraits. The most beautiful of the chapels is that beside the south end of the crossing, the Gothic Chapel of St Wenceslas. This is founded on the same site as the Saint's original grave. The lower part of the wall is encrusted with over 1,300 pieces of jasper and amethyst, above which are wall paintings executed between 1372 and 1373. The Czechoslovak coronation jewels may be seen in a chamber which is reached via a portal in the wall below the window of the chapel.

In front of the High Altar is the royal Renaissance tomb, made for Ferdinand I, with his son Maximilian on his right and his consort Anna Jagellon on his left, of white marble. The New Archbishops' chapel contains the coloured window, designed by Alfons Mucha, illustrating the legends of patron saints.

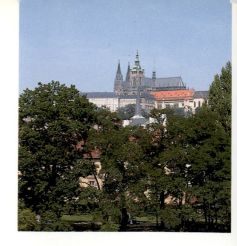

The beautiful Cathedral of St Vitus overlooks the city of Prague

Prato, Italy

Originally consisting of just a nave and a small choir, the 13th century Cathedral at Prato was expanded in 1317, when a transept was added and the choir enlarged under the supervision of Giovanni Pisano, whose work brought together the separate parts to create one of the most harmonious churches in Tuscany. In the 15th century Gothic additions were made to the white and green façade, Donatello made reliefs, della Robbia fashioned enamelled terracottas and Fra Filippo

One of Prato's outstanding features is the external pulpit, which is situated in the south west corner of the west front

ppi painted frescoes. There is also a chapel dedicated to the Holy Girdle of the Virgin, a relic reportedly handed to the Apostle Thomas by the Virgin after her Assumption.

Reims, France

Reims has had a Christian cathedral since 401, when St Nicasius dedicated a pagan temple to Mary. There followed a succession of basilicas and churches on the site, and by the early 13th century the last of these had burnt down. This provided an ideal excuse for the then Bishop of Reims, Albéric de Humbert, to build his own Cathedral. As he had been archdeacon at Nôtre Dame in Paris, it is not surprising that Nôtre Dame in Reims should follow its namesake in many respects, particularly in the façade of the cathedral. However, true kings of France have been crowned at Reims since the late fifth century, and the Cathedral is to the French as Canterbury is to the English.

Virtually complete by the end of the 13th century, the Cathedral is one of rare beauty. The choir, transepts, nave and towers had all been finished and the great rose window was in place above the main portal.

The west front of Reims, displaying many of the statues for which it is famous

Just 30 years later, the carvings and statuary which cover the cathedral were also complete; there are over 5,000 statues of bishops, kings, saints, devils, knights, vassals and craftsmen.

Despite having been heavily bombed in 1914 and 1918, the structure remained and the Cathedral was restored after the War was over, standing proudly once again to represent the sacred centre of the French nation.

Rome (St Peter's), Italy

The shrine of the first of the Apostles, St Peter, is second only to the Holy Sepulchre in Jerusalem among the churches of Christendom. Founded in about 322 by Constantine the

Great, it was substantially complete within 15 years, but it was not until the 15th century when the Papal Curia was established in Rome that it gained its modern importance.

The foundations had been laid over a pagan cemetery, the shrine beneath the High Altar dating from the year 170. In 800, Pope Leo III founded the Holy Roman Empire by crowning Charlemagne Emperor of the West there; but over the next 650 years, St Peter's gradually had fallen into decay, until a new project was conceived by Pope Nicholas V. In 1450 plans were prepared to provide a worthy successor, and the first stone of the present St Peter's was laid on 18 April 1506.

To its original simple and majestic concept of a Greek cross covered by a huge central dome with four smaller domes at the sides, successive architects added chapels and also confused the plan by stretching the nave and the eastern arm of the transept, thereby creating a plan more like a Latin cross.

The interior's wondrous beauty is due to Michelangelo's masterly treatment of scale. The erection of the drum of the cupola, which was accomplished in his lifetime and the cupola, which was built from designs left by him, are gen-erally regarded as one of the supreme masterpieces of world architecture. The nave and façade were both designed by Maderna and choir stalls by Bernini, who had also designed the Piazza in front of the Cathedral.

St Alban's, England

Long and narrow, with its massive central tower, St Alban's is the highest English cathedral, having been built some 97.5m (320ft) above sea level. In origin it is an early Norman building, and the nave, at 83.3m (275ft) is one of the longest medieval naves in existence. The tower, with its striking arcade, is constructed largely of Roman bricks and tiles.

Founded by Otta of Mercia around 793 as a Benedictine monastery, it was largely re-built between 1077 and 1155 by Abbot Paul of Caen, and was elevated to cathedral status in 1877.

The plan of St Alban's forms a simple cross with a plain and graceful west end and a nave which is separated from the choir by a stone rood screen of 1350. The nave has rather austere piers, contrasting with the central tower at its inter-section.

On the west and south sides of the Norman piers are remnants of 13th and 14th century wall paintings, including one which is thought to be the work of Walter of Colchester, of c1220. On the wall of the south aisle are four colourful embroidery panels, depicting the religious significance of Earth, Air, Fire and Water.

A fine ceiling over the choir dates from the late 15th century, and the magnificent brass of Abbot Thomas de la Mare (d 1396) is in the south choir aisle. The Cathedral also houses the shrine of St Alban and the tomb of a brother of Henry V, Duke Humphrey of Gloucester (d 1447).

Mary and the dead Christ in the Chapel of St Carmona, which is entered via the Chapel of San José in the new Cathedral

Salamanca, Spain

There are two cathedrals at Salamanca, which together throw up a veritable thicket of spiky spires and turrets into the sky. The Old Cathedral is entered through the new, the *Catedral Nueva*, which was begun in 1512; its nave was followed by the transept in 1538, when the nave was completed. Work on the dome was started as recently as 1705, and the Cathedral was completed in 1759. The entire building measures 124m (407ft) in length, 60m (197ft) in width and has a span of 13m (43ft), a height of 35.3m (116ft), and a tower 110m (361ft) high.

Regarded as Gothic's last gasp, though Baroque and Plateresque elements were added, the west façade is a study in arches upon arches, which are embellished with coats of arms, statues and reliefs. Inside there are three naves, some quite outstanding Baroque choir stalls and a beautifully maintained 18th century organ. There are no less than 18 side chapels, including the Golden Chapel, where there are 110 sculptures.

Other important works include a 13th century Virgin in gilt-bronze, a Byzantine crucifix that was carried into battle by *El Cid*, and some 16th century Flemish glass.

The *Catedral Vieja* is not so grand, though the smaller size conveys a far more intimate feeling. The Cathedral, which was begun in the 12th century, contains a main altar with 53 paintings by Nicholas of Florence; highlighting a statue of the Virgin above the retable is Nicholas' very dramatic and detailed Last Judgment.

The cloister here is a replacement of the 18th century for the original, which was destroyed as a result of the distant Lisbon earthquake of 1755.

Segovia, Spain

The last of the great Gothic cathedrals, not only in Spain but throughout all the world, Segovia is set well up on a hill within the old city, and visible from all around. Its generous proportions and finely finished masonry are perfectly complemented by its Gothic pinnacles.

The plan is symmetrically laid out and proportioned by rule. It has three aisles as well as external cellular chapels, a chevet of seven chapels sur-

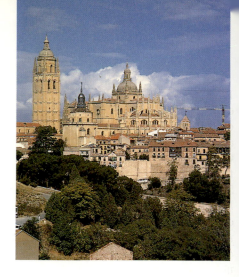

The Cathedral of Segovia was designed in 1525 by Juan Gil de Hontañón but not finished until the end of the 17th century

rounding an ambulatory, an eastern arm of one square bay, a transept which does not extend beyond the outer walls and five bays of nave. Internally each bay of vaulting is marked off by cross-arches giving each an independent appearance. The great tower was struck by lightning in 1614, and lost 6.7m (22ft) from its height.

Fine stained glass windows illuminate the church, and show the majestic columns to their best; remarkably, there are also two magnificent 18th century organs.

Right: *the Cathedral seen from the approaches to Siena; Pisano's pulpit is illustrated on page 21*

Siena, Italy

It was decided to replace the earlier cathedral at Siena with one worthy of the Commune and Republic of Siena in 1226. Collections were made among the citizens to raise funds, and 50 years later the Romanesque basilica was complete. Some considerable alterations were undertaken in the early years of the 14th century, including the rebuilding of the east end, which was extended by four bays beyond the cupola; the heightening of the nave roofs; and the addition of the lower stage of the façade. The transept was also enlarged, and the baptistery became the crypt. The Cathedral was enlarged further by work beginning in 1339, but sadly the finances that were then available were insufficient and the work was abandoned, leaving the south side of the transept incomplete.

The tall narrow splayed windows of the aisle walls, the elaborate doorway in the east wall and the vigorous abundant carvings of the capitals and corbels, along with the careful overall arrangement of the cornices, friezes and the courses of black and white marble, demonstrate the thought and care that had gone into the creation of the Cathedral from the very beginning, and it remains a pity that the undertaking has never been completed.

The rose windows are filled with the deep colours of stained glass; the pavement is unique for the extent and beauty of its rare marble inlay. Little of the medieval furniture remains beyond Nicola Pisano's renowned pulpit, which is the most important single work of art in the Cathedral.

Speyer, Germany

The Kaiserdom is one of the largest medieval churches in Europe, certainly one of the finest Romanesque cathedrals, and a building that more than any other in Germany conveys the pomp and majesty of the early Holy Roman emperors. It was built in only 30 years, in between 1030 and 1060, by the emperors Konrad II, Heinrich III and Heinrich IV. A four year

restoration programme in the 1950s returned the building almost exactly to its condition when first completed. Speyer Cathedral, thanks chiefly to the fact that later ages never saw fit to rebuild it, and partly to the intelligent restoration of the 1950s, embodies all that is best in Romanesque architecture.

Speyer Cathedral appears a much more massive building when compared to the one at Köln, especially when viewed from the park next to the Rhine, which affords an excellent view. The few windows are small, with the round tops characteristic of their style. There are four towers, two at each end, and an immense smoothly curving dome at the east end, which gives the building a distinctive profile. Having been built all at one time, the church remains faithful to a single vision.

At Speyer the columns supporting the roof are massive, their bulk naturally obscuring the side aisles, drawing the eye to the altar. The nave roof is a shallow stone vault, the very earliest such vaulted roof in Europe. The richly carved capitals of the columns are filled with lively naturalistic details of foliage, animals, birds, and human faces.

No less than eight Holy Roman emperors are buried in the Cathedral, including the three founders, who lie in the crypt.

Tarazona, Spain

Tarazona is a picturesque mountain town, some 80km (50 miles) WNW of Zaragoza in the lower reaches of the Sierra de Moncayo, with the Cathedral standing at the base of a hill. Its most remarkable feature is its unique serried central lantern, which is far more complex than others such as that at *La Seo*, Zaragoza, even though it was designed by the same master, Juan Botero. The buttresses of the main stage have two series of pinnacles, with pillared openwork caps, and above this rise two further stages instead of one.

The rest of the structure is built in a mixture of styles and rebuildings and repairs, and these have resulted in the most intriguing and charming of cloisters. Structurally it is late Gothic and built of brick, the buttressed piers towards the garth having inlaid patterns of part-Gothic and part-mudéjar style; but the pointed arches between them are filled with an elaborate screen work of stone pierced in filigree patterns.

Tours, France

The present St Gatien's Cathedral at Tours succeeds three former churches. The first of these, built by St Lidoire, had been replaced by a Frankish church with mosaics in honour of St Martin and stood for 400 years. The third church, which was Romanesque, was soon destroyed by fire, having stood for barely a century.

The new church was Gothic, and in spite of a good start to the building work with the completion of the chancel after 40 years, it took another three

The apse is illustrated on page 7; below is one of the apsidal chapels, with the window of the Covenant of Tours Cathedral

centuries to complete, and the styles range from early to late Gothic, together with some Renaissance.

The transepts were finished in the 14th century, and the soaring nave, begun early in the same century, was completed and vaulted in the 15th century. The façade, with its three lavishly embellished portals, shows the unfettered opulence of the late form Flamboyant period. Stained glass windows from the various periods of construction add brilliance and colour to the interior.

Externally the apse is one of the finest in Gothic style at its height, rising gently and harmoniously. The double flighted buttresses seem to raise it up, the slanting angle providing both movement and variety.

Valladolid, Spain

The Cathedral at Valladolid was not begun until 1580, although the foundations were started in 1527, and it was 1595 before it was made the seat of a bishop. Designed by Juan de Herrera, nevertheless it ranks among the most important in Spain, if for no other reason than its huge size; 137m (450ft) in length, 72m (236ft) wide and with a span of 15m (49ft). However, it is a cold, solemn and unfinished building, somewhat out of place in this charming royal city, which also boasts of having Spain's first university. Inside the Cathedral there are many works of art, the highlight of which is an altarpiece by Juan de Juni.

Venice, Italy

St Mark's was begun in 828, as a resting place for the remains of the city's patron saint, and as the private chapel of the Doge. In 976, it was set on fire by the populace in protest against the power of the doges but it was quickly restored, and in 1063 considerably enlarged; the new building was consecrated in 1094. This new structure had been modelled on the cruciform pattern of Constantinople's Church of the Holy Apostles, with a mighty central dome surmounting the intersection of the Greek cross with four smaller cupolas marking its extremities.

St Mark's differs from all other great churches, not only in the unity of its unusual structure, but also in the magnificence of its internal and external decorations. The brilliant contrast of the coloured marble and mosaic pictures with the strong shadows of the

One of St Mark's cupolas, in the late afternoon sunshine

deep recesses, the robust arches below the fretted pinnacles and weird onion-shaped cupolas above emphasise the unique place that the basilica holds in European architecture.

The interior also has a rare splendour, despite the rather excessive marble decoration and poor light. Some 4,180m² (5,000sq yd) of glass mosaic in bright colours on a lustrous gold ground cover the immense superficial area of the walls and cupolas, a work that was completed in the 14th century. These embellishments have survived largely intact, though some pictures were replaced during the 16th and 17th centuries.

Vitoria, Spain

The *Catedral Nueva*, which is in the modern city is a large neo Gothic construction begun in 1906, in marked contrast to the ancient *Colegiata de Santa María* which was built some six centuries earlier. The style of the latter is Navarrese, and results from the occupation of Vitoria from 1366 to 1413 by the Kings of Navarre.

It has a fine central portal to the main west front flanked by statues, with a tympanum elaborately carved in four scenes of the life of the Virgin. The richly moulded orders of the surrounding arch are provided with two series of statues in niches, following the curve, and foliage is carried round the main arch and the doorways. However, far more exciting is its central mullion, bearing a standing figure of the Virgin, which closely resembles Our Lady of Succour in the cloister of Pamplona.

Inside there is a three aisled nave, with five bays, a wide transept of three bays on each side, and a five sided central apse opening immediately off the crossing and surrounded by three hexagonal chapels and the trapezoidal chapels of the east side of the transept.

Wells, England

The Saxon church of St Andrew was founded at Wells in 704, by King Ine of Wessex, near a natural spring from which the city takes its name. In 909 the episcopal see was established by Edward the Elder and when this was transferred to Bath by Bishop John de Villula Wells fell into ruin.

In 1135, Robert of Lewes had become Bishop, rebuilding most of the cathedral in the Norman style, but the building was torn down when Bishop Reginald de Bohun began construction of the present Gothic Cathedral around 1180, with its glorious west front with its wide screen of over 300 statues. There were originally over 400 figures in full colour, a summation of sacred and profane history, in six tiers carried over the whole façade and round the sides of the west towers. The three west bays of the choir, the transepts and the east bays of the nave were all probably finished soon after 1200, before the nave and west front. The church was consecrated in 1239.

During the Protestant Reformation in the 17th century, the church was plundered, the Lady Chapel destroyed, much of the See's land seized by the Duke of Somerset, who stripped the

The Wells scissor arch

lead from the windows.

Wells is not a large cathedral, but is among the most beautiful and complete in England. Its most unusual feature is its very large 14th century inverted double arch or scissor arch dedicated to St Andrew, built to strengthen the crossing. The Heavenly Stair, which leads to the chapter house and to the gallery over the choir is early Decorated in style, exquisite and time worn.

From the south transept a staircase climbs the central tower 55.5m (182ft) and also leads to the chapter library, built over the east walk of the cloisters in 1425. It contains 6,000 books, original charters from 958 onwards and a crozier decorated with Limoges enamel of the 13th century.

Winchester, England

In 634 Bishop Birinus, while on a mission from Rome, came to Britain to undertake the conversion of the West Saxons. Egbert was crowned king at Winchester in 828 as was Alfred in 871, and had his kingdom been perpetuated by his successors, Winchester rather than London would have become the centre of British government.

The present church fabric was begun in 1079 by Bishop Walkelyn, William's cousin, after the Norman Conquest. He had erected a church in the Norman style, but in 1107, the central tower fell in onto the tomb of William Rufus, who had recently been buried there. Further structural alterations were made to the Norman church before Godfrey de Lucy tore down its east end and rebuilt it in Early English style. The nave was converted from Norman to Perpendicular style in the 14th century and between 1487 and 1493 the Bishop Peter Courtenay added a bay to the east end and made Winchester the longest church in England.

The 12th century font in the north aisle is made from black marble from Tournai, France, and is rich in carvings. The choir is separated from the nave by an oak screen designed by Sir George Gilbert Scott. The stalls are magnificent; their misericords, carved with human, animal and monster motifs, are the oldest cathedral stalls in England except for some fragments at Rochester. The crypt is impressive, though subject to flooding in the winter months; there is a well under the High Altar.

The Winchester Bible of the 12th century is a magnificent illuminated Vulgate (Latin Bible) in four volumes. It was rebound in 1948, and is in the chapter house library, which also contains 4,000 printed books and some rare manuscripts.

Xanten, Germany

The city's name is derived from the Latin *ad Sanctos Martyres* via Santen, and the Cathedral crypt contains the original cell of the Cathedral and the city. Here lie two tombs of early Christian martyrs, Christians and soldiers of the Theban Legion during the time of the Roman occupation of the Rhineland, from 361 to 363. These untouched tombs below the crypt were found during the archaeological excavations in 1933. The same excavations also confirmed that a church had been erected above the tombs, and the foundation of a chapter in the eighth century, the canons of which cared for the tombs and the church. The medieval town of Xanten had developed round its Cathedral, the cloister walk, the chapter buildings and the residences of the chapter, all of which offered sanctuary.

Today the crypt remains a most relevant and moving memorial, as to commemorate the victims who died there, since 1966 it has been a resting place of some earth gathered from the concentration camps of Auschwitz, Bergen-Belsen and Dachau. By perpetuating the memory of those who have died as a result of their beliefs rather than submit to tyranny, over a period of 1600 years, the congregation of Xanten has created a lasting act of homage which both humbly and most generously transcends any sectarian schisms.

The foundation stone of the present Gothic Cathedral was laid in 1263. The final building, which had followed six earlier churches, connected to the Romanesque west front and was completed around 1520. Only the choir stalls, the oldest in the Rhineland, of 1221 to 1226, and the shrine of St Victor (1129) near the gable of the new

High Altar have been retained from the fittings of the early Romanesque church.

Karl Leisner, prisoner no 22356

Born in 1915, he joined Christ's Youth at grammar school and graduated in 1934. He first studied for the priesthood at Munster, and was entrusted with leading the Catholic boys' youth group of the diocese, finishing his studies at Freiberg.

He became a sub-deacon on 4 March 1939, and a deacon on 25 March 1939, but before he took holy orders was arrested by the Gestapo because of the remark he made regarding the assassination attempt on Hitler on 8 November 1939.

Imprisoned in Freiberg, he was committed to Sachsenhausen, and then in December 1940 to Dachau. When he fell ill from tuberculosis, Bishop Gabriel Piguet, a French prisoner, then administered the ordination for Leisner on 17 December 1944. Liberation was on 4 May 1945, but Leisner died on 12 August 1945, having made a final entry in his diary on 25 June, which reads: 'Bless also, Greatest One, my enemies'. His grave is in the martyrs' crypt at Xanten, and on 15 March 1980 Pope John Paul II gave permission to open the proceedings of beatification.

Zamora, Spain

Despite its military position as a key border site fortified againsts the incursion of the Moors, Zamora became a strong centre of the Christian faith. The Cathedral, built in the 12th century, was probably the most notable religious structure in León and Castile at the time, harmoniously combining a Romanesque ground plan with an Oriental lantern dome over the crossing. The latter was completely new to any contemporaneous Spanish Romanesque architecture, and is believed to have been an importation from either the Latin Kingdom of Jerusalem or from the Byzantine Empire. The central dome is set in a

The dome of Zamora Cathedral, with its fish scale tiles; ruins of the old city wall may be seen in the foreground

cluster of four smaller cupolas, and is covered in scalloped fish-scale tiles, but the building is dominated by a massive three storey martial tower which remains unfinished.

One outstanding feature of the Cathedral is the door on the south façade, *Puerta del Obispo* facing the bishop's palace. The door, with its floral motifs, is flanked by a pair of blind doors, one of which is surmounted by a particularly fine relief which depicts the Virgin and Child with angels.

Zaragoza, Spain

Zaragoza is the capital of Aragón, and stands on Spain's greatest river, the Ebro. It has two cathedrals; to the west the Basilica of Nuestra Señora del Pilár (Our Lady of the Pillar), begun in 1509 stands, backing onto the Ebro. A little over 200m (656ft) away stands the old *La Seo* Cathedral, which began its existence as a mosque. Although it has been almost completely remodelled over the centuries, traces of its Moorish origins can be seen in a section of the exterior wall, decorated with a typical brick and tile mosaic, and in the square floor plan of the interior. It has been closed for a number of years for renovation and to allow the extensive excavation of the earlier Roman baths beneath, which now form a permanent exhibition entered from outside the Cathedral. *La Seo* has five aisles and side chapels inside, including one dedicated to SS Peter and Paul, with the central nave slightly higher than the aisles. It has a decorative open wrought iron screen enclosing the choir, and an alabaster altarpiece in the main chapel. The chapter house contains many fine paintings by Goya, Ribera and Zurbarán.

By contrast, the Basilica gives a general impression of un-European exoticism, with its orange-brown brick and roofs of coloured tiles in patterns. There are four corner towers, though only two of these are finished and in size it ranks among Spain's largest, being 132.5m (435ft) long, 67m (22ft) wide and with a span of 15.8m (52ft). Bright and always packed with pilgrims, it contains a small Gothic statue of Spain's patron saint. Legend maintains that the Virgin Mary appeared here in the year 40, standing on a jasper pillar. The basilica has been built around the column, which is available for pilgrims to kiss at the back of the elaborate Capilla de Pilár.

ACKNOWLEDGMENTS

Superlaunch Ltd is indebted to John Anstey for permission to use the pictures of English cathedrals on pages 40, 44, 56 (inset); 64 (main picture) and 92; and also thanks Carole Ismay for additional photography, and Andrew Wright for the artworks which appear on pages 8 and 9

The Berliner Dom is currently being renovated; when I last visited Berlin, the cross above the south door was being hoisted into position, but in the autumn of 1994, a fire caused extensive damage, which will delay the reopening until 1997. This view is of the west front